C

D0266988

UNION J

UNION J

EMILY HERBERT

OMNIBUS PRESS

London / New York / Paris / Sydney / Copenhagen / Berlin / Madrid / Tokyo

Copyright © 2013 Omnibus Press
(A Division of Music Sales Limited)

Cover designed by Fresh Lemon
Picture research by Jacqui Black

ISBN: 978.1.78035.153.3
Order No: OP55451

The Author hereby asserts his/her right to be identified as the author of
this work in accordance with Sections 77 to 78 of the Copyright,
Designs and Patents Act 1988.

All rights reserved. No part of this book may be reproduced in any
form or by any electronic or mechanical means, including information
storage or retrieval systems, without permission in writing from the
publisher, except by a reviewer who may quote brief passages.

Exclusive Distributors
Music Sales Limited,
14/15 Berners Street,
London, W1T 3LJ.

Music Sales Corporation,
257 Park Avenue South,
New York, NY 10010, USA.

Macmillan Distribution Services,
56 Parkwest Drive
Derrimut, Vic 3030,
Australia.

Every effort has been made to trace the copyright holders of the
photographs in this book but one or two were unreachable. We would
be grateful if the photographers concerned would contact us.

Printed in the EU

A catalogue record for this book is available from the British Library.

Visit Omnibus Press on the web at www.omnibuspress.com

Contents

1

Three Becomes Four

Caroline Flack had a good idea.

The 30-something presenter of *The Xtra Factor*, the supplementary show that aired after the hugely popular and long-running *The X Factor*, had just seen a promising outfit called Triple J booted off the ninth series of the programme. Yet she still had an inkling that they may have a bright future after all.

Why not take another of the contestants, George Shelley, and put him in the line-up of the band? He was young, personable, had a great voice and would fit in well with the others. It would also make great television, as a precedent had already been set. Caroline had a ringside seat at the proceedings when One Direction had originally entered *The X Factor* as five solo artists, to be told, famously, that they had a better future as a group. She had also enjoyed a brief and extremely public liaison with one prominent member of One Direction, Harry Styles, so who better than Caroline to figure just how well this might turn out?

That, at any rate, is the 'official' version of the story as revealed through footage of *The Xtra Factor* – although some commentators have claimed it was all down to *X Factor* judge Louis Walsh. After all, Caroline was a TV presenter whereas Louis was a hugely canny music mogul who had been in the industry for most of his life. He was more than able to spot potential when it stepped out of nowhere, particularly if it came in the shape of four young men who would make a great boy band.

Walsh himself also had a personal motive to look for new talent, of which more anon. In truth, it was far more likely that the burst of inspiration that would have such an impact on show business was his. But the mystery surrounding who came up with the original idea was pure *X Factor*: with its squabbling judges, diva-like behaviour, tiffs, spats, rows and very public triumphs, it had been producing stars on a regular basis and was about to do so yet again.

There is a mysterious alchemy to *The X Factor* that can take totally different entrants and transform them into a major star unit. Originally, all of the group had been presented in a totally different format: Triple J was a three-piece outfit, consisting of Josh Thomas John Cuthbert, Jamie Paul 'JJ' Hamblett and James William Jaymi Hensley (hence Triple J – all their names begin with 'J', geddit?); the slightly younger Shelley had entered the show as a solo act. But there was a link between him and Triple J, in that they all shared Blair Dreelan as a manager. This was to make life a lot easier as they all got used to one another in the early days – after all, everyone's expectations had already been turned on their heads.

But it was not just an inspired piece of blue-sky thinking that gave Union J their lucky break. Triple J had failed to make it through the 'Boot Camp' stage of the show, before proceedings moved on to the 'Judges' Houses' slot. This was the segment when each judge mentors a different type of contestant. This year, Louis Walsh was going to be looking after the groups: Triple J had previously sung with fellow entrants GMD3 in a battle for the slot, but their rivals had triumphed; another group to get through was an outfit from south London called Rough Copy.

However, with just a few days to go before everyone was due to fly out to work with Louis in Las Vegas, it emerged that a member of Rough Copy had visa problems. Nigerian-born Kazeem Ajobo had applied for a visa that would allow him to travel to the States and then return to the UK, but it would not be ready in time for the band to travel to Vegas. There was no bar to him leaving the country – but no guarantee he would be allowed back in. Much to his own and everyone else's disappointment, Rough Copy were forced to withdraw from the competition – although there were hopes they'd have another go at it the following year.

This created total pandemonium behind the scenes at *The X Factor*. Someone had to come up with a new plan, fast. Louis Walsh stepped up to bat: he would replace Rough Copy with not one but two alternatives, Triple J and Times Red, another of the bands in the show. It was a surprise but it looked as if it might work: "When Rough Copy left, I found it difficult to choose between two groups to fill their place," he told the *Daily Mirror*. "In the end I invited boy band Triple J to come to Judges' Houses, but still felt that as I'd lost such a strong group in Rough Copy that I wanted to make sure the category was the best it could possibly be. I asked [fellow judges] Gary, Nicole and Tulisa if they minded if I took a seventh act. They were happy as they felt they'd got the right six acts for their Judges' Houses trips so I asked Times Red to come along and they said yes."

As with Louis Walsh, Gary Barlow, Nicole Scherzinger and Tulisa Contostavlos were all well aware that teasing the public by overturning rules and introducing surprise factors was bound to make for great television. And so Triple J found themselves back in the game once more. .

However, there was still a small problem. Triple J hadn't made it through previously because the act hadn't seemed quite right, giving Caroline, or Louis (or an unnamed executive working in the background), the bright idea of adding a new member to the existing line-up. Three was an odd number for a boy band, anyway – they tended to work better with four or five, which gave fans a bigger choice to pick out their favourite, as well as providing some kind of insurance should one band member quit. If someone left a boy band with three members, that turned the remaining two into a double act, whereas five could very successfully slim down to four – as Take That had so famously demonstrated.

As George was both personable and talented, why not give it a go? By this stage, none of them had anything to lose anyway. It seemed like the perfect way to forge ahead.

In fact the boys had already formed an initial bond. They had discovered in the earlier stages of the show that they could get along, which would be crucial not only to their performance in *The X Factor* but (with any luck) in the years ahead. If they had been four boys with no chemistry between them, it would have shown up in their body language, which would be hugely off-putting to the fans. It might have created rivalries and tensions, given that band members are forced to spend a huge amount of time together in the recording studio and out on the road. Triple J might also have resented the intrusion of a new-comer – though that was most certainly *not* the case.

"George loved the idea and as the boys knew him from Boot Camp they were really happy for him to join them," Louis Walsh told the *Daily Mirror*. "The group then came up with a new name and they are now called Union J." It went without saying that everyone involved was delighted – they were getting a new lease of life. After the stunning success of One Direction a couple of years previously, everyone knew what kind of rewards were on offer for the right outfit. Music industry wisdom had it that there was always room for another boy band and, if handled really well, it could become a highly lucrative career. The conventional wisdom also had it that boy bands only had a couple of years at the top of the tree, but this had been turned on its head by the astonishing example of Take That. Having also been a manufactured band of five strangers brought together by one wily manager, after their initial split in the nineties and their subsequent comeback (and transformation into national treasures), Take That had made it plain that this could be a long-lived career.

Of course, Louis Walsh, as a veteran of the pop industry, also had a particular interest in boy bands. Born in Kiltimagh, County Mayo, he had first moved to Dublin and then to London to work within the music industry, gaining a long history of appearing on TV talent shows along the way. Walsh had first appeared, in 2001, in the Irish version of *Popstars*; the following year he moved to UK television for *Popstars: The Rivals*, on ITV. He would have an on-off relationship with *The X Factor* from its first appearance in 2004, as one of the original judges alongside Simon Cowell and Sharon Osbourne. Although various spats had prompted him to take the odd break from the show, by 2012 he'd been well and truly ensconced in the programme for a long time. Louis knew what made good television; he could also pick talent when he saw it, and he could see there was real potential there.

In fact, Louis Walsh was one of the most experienced people in the industry when it came to realising the potential of boy bands. By now in his early sixties, he'd had an astronomically successful career managing Johnny Logan, Boyzone and Westlife, three of the most successful acts to have emerged from Ireland. And, while there was always room for another boy band to meet a fresh generation of fans, this was an especially propitious moment: Westlife, who had enjoyed a stratospherically successful career, had just announced they were splitting up after a career spanning 14 years.

In its day, Westlife had sold over 50 million records worldwide, with 14 number one singles in the UK alone (the third highest placings, tying with Cliff Richard and coming in behind The Beatles and Elvis Presley). If there was any chance at all that a similar situation could be created with Union J, then there was everything to play for. None of the emerging groups of this period were being hailed as replacements for older outfits per se, but there was a loose sense that, if One Direction were to be the next Take That, then Union J had at least a chance of emulating the success of Westlife.

From early on, the boys had clearly begun to engage the public's attention. A considerable amount of media coverage surrounded the decision to incorporate George into the new band, always a sure sign that a particular set-up is standing out from the crowd. The boys also began to give interviews, small hints at what was going on behind the scenes. As Jaymi said to *Now* magazine: "We have got a girl band of mums supporting us. My sister cried so much during auditions, she passed out! All the nans like Josh. We are such mummy's boys. If we had a big party with loads of models, our mums would be there, putting clothes on all the models."

It wasn't exactly hard-living rock'n'roll, but it was a charming picture to paint. It did the boys no harm at all, establishing the likelihood that they would appeal to an older generation. There had been some amusement about the fact that One Direction was not just appealing to teenage girls but to their mothers as well, but if the same could be achieved for Union J then it doubled the potential fan base – and possibly trebled the profits that came not just from music sales, but from touring and associated merchandise. There was big money to be made for a band which caught the public's attention in such a way.

According to *Unreality TV*, the boys "insisted that there will be no mad partying, no excessive drinking and no illegal drug taking" as the programme wore on. It was not necessarily the attitude you would expect a bunch of high-spirited teenage boys to come out with, but it highlighted the fact that this was one boy band that would present itself as squeaky clean.

(Take That had made a similar public show of sobriety and self-control two decades previously – although it was later revealed that all was not quite what it seemed behind the scenes.)

Elsewhere, there were comments to the effect that George bore some resemblance to Harry Styles – one fan "wrote this story about me [saying] I'm the child of Harry and Liam from One Direction," he quipped, while *Independent Voice* made a more cynical comment: "George was foisted on them by the ruthless money-making algorithms of the record industry." Those 'ruthless money-making algorithms' seemed to know their stuff, however, as Union J was shaping up very well indeed for a new band.

Serious comparisons with One Direction have carried on to the present day, but the truth is that it's not so much how Union J physically resemble their *X Factor* predecessors, as that every one of them possesses characteristics that are a crucial ingredient of every successful boy band. Although all four of them are strikingly good looking, none of them are overtly masculine in

13

a way that fans might find threatening. There is no hint of hairiness (and they would be well advised to keep it that way); no beards or bulging biceps; nothing that would hint of life as, say, a biker rather than a pop star. Chest hair, if it existed, had been expunged. Everything about them glowed, from their cleanly brushed teeth to their scrupulously tidy fingernails. It may sound trivial, but a lot depends on details even as small as those.

Almost every teen idol, from Donny Osmond and David Cassidy, in the seventies, through Wham! (George Michael is virtually unrecognisable as the same man), New Kids On The Block, Westlife and Take That in its earlier incarnation had a slightly androgynous quality that young girls find appealing. Union J is no exception to that rule. Clean-shaven, lively and looking younger than their years, they could not have looked more like the ideal boy band. They knew it, and so did their behind-the-scenes stylists. The boys were now beginning to receive advice on everything from what they said in public to the minute details of their appearance. By this stage, as their potential became ever more obvious, nothing was being left to chance.

Meanwhile, One Direction responded to the potential competition graciously: Louis Tomlinson tweeted how pleased he was that the boys got through and, indeed, they would go on to meet him. Harry Styles lost no time in showing that he, too, was unfazed by the new boys, who were "really great and talented acts". The One Direction boys were only in their late teens and early twenties, but already they were old hands, veterans of the show business world. How long would it take Union J to find themselves in the same position?

Their presentation was spot-on. All four (like One Direction) favoured the preppy look: T-shirts combined with jeans or chinos; plimsolls but rarely trainers; sometimes jackets, sometimes trousers rolled up to display a bit of leg. Several sported 'interesting' haircuts in the One Direction mode. It was stylish without being über-fashionable, casual, relaxed and promoting the image of a very, very good-looking boy next door. The one exception to the decades-old squeaky-clean rule was tattoos: the odd ink stain was in evidence, as Harry Styles had already proven that it didn't matter any more.

Louis Walsh clearly believed that they knew exactly what they were doing: "The boys have a great young image," he told the *Mail Online*. "Girls are going to love them, they have it all – great energy, looks and vocals to match." The girls were already beginning to love them, if fan sites were anything to go by. The buzz began to build. Union J was clearly the Next Big Thing.

The boys themselves were understandably wary of any comparisons – if they failed to make the grade, it all risked blowing up in their faces at this very early stage. As for One Direction, that was a very big act to follow and it often made them uncomfortable when the comparison was made. "Um, we're a four-piece, they're a five . . . No, we do different music. We're just different," Josh told *Heat* magazine. "They're very young-poppy. We're a bit like Maroon 5. I'm not sure it's possible to be any bigger than One Direction, but that would be amazing – that would be the dream."

His caution was understandable, but it was clear that something was beginning to gel. They continued to attract much female attention, something that had not been so marked in the earlier stages of the show. As the *Radio Times* had remarked in its regular commentary on *The X Factor*: "Union J are a One Direction with vocals, who are dark horses for the whole thing." That might have been true early on, but those dark horses were increasingly edging into the limelight.

The boys were loving it, of course, but it was an awful lot to take onboard. One of the drawbacks to becoming a star via reality television is that there is no adjustment time; whereas bands who have to slog around the circuit get used to dealing with the attention over a period of months, or even years, reality stars have to go from totally unknown to a huge star sometimes overnight. The best example of this is Susan Boyle, who ended up for a brief period in the Priory clinic when she found it hard to cope.

Even though the boys were not yet pitched into that level of fame, some adjustments to their thinking had to be made. In addition, they were attracting more attention than they might have done otherwise because of the way they had been put together. Unlike most manufactured bands (in other words, the vast majority of bands who become successful), even their very creation had been the subject of publicity, and, of course, there was also social media to deal with. The boys were gaining an increasingly high profile, which meant that they were getting recognised with some regularity. It was a foretaste of the huge amount of attention to come.

But the early indications were that it was all going well, partic-ularly the tricky aspect of manoeuvring a newcomer into an already established band. Shortly after Union J was formed, the boys appeared on *Daybreak*, where they revealed that everything was going very much to plan. "It's been awesome," Jaymi said of George's arrival in the group. "He just fitted in straight away. He's just one of us now. It was funny, because we'd become quite good friends with him at Boot Camp, and for him to be put in was wicked."

George clearly agreed. "These guys are like my brothers now," he said. "We have spent so much time together. It's wicked. We have had to practise. Obviously the other groups have been together longer than us, so we've had to put in extra work, but hopefully it will pay off."

It already was, given the frequency with which the boys were now appearing in the media. The only unimpressed party, funnily enough, was the bookies, who were not offering good odds on the boys winning – but then it didn't matter if they didn't take the number one slot. One Direction didn't actually win *The X Factor*, nor did Susan Boyle win *Britain's Got Talent*; in neither case did it exactly hold them back. What mattered about these TV shows was national exposure, making contacts in the industry and showing potential. In that way, *The X Factor* really was just like an old-fashioned audition: the difference being that it was watched by millions, not just a couple of casting directors. Union J was being called upon to show that they could operate as a successful modern pop group.

The local press in the various locations that the boys had sprung from were becoming interested too, drumming up facts about their past lives and urging support of the local boys. There was a definite curiosity about where they'd come from and what they'd been doing until now – the fact that JJ already had public exposure in an early period as a jockey was much commented upon, with figures from the racing world brought out to have their say.

And so the scene was set. The makers of *The X Factor* had yet again pulled off a coup: they had presented the viewers with something totally unexpected, creating a mini-drama about personable young men whose hopes had been dashed, only to be dramatically revived. It got the whole nation talking about these boys who had apparently sprung from nowhere.

And the boys themselves? They were well aware of what was

at stake and knew they had been presented with an opportunity they should avoid messing up. All had some experience of show business in the past, to a greater or lesser extent, and knew it was a tough old world they were taking on. Whatever happened next, they had to give it their all; if they didn't seize it with both hands, there was no guarantee they would get such a chance again.

And so they buckled down, going in to rehearsals, getting the act together and trying to ignore the increasingly heavy weight of expectation on their shoulders. Very few people got even as far as they had done to date, and yet they were still at the very beginning. The real trials of strength and endurance were yet to come.

2

How It All Began

Rewind to July 2011.

Julian White had decided the time was right to start a boy band. A veteran of the music industry, he'd started out working for his father, Bruce White, the founder of Creole Records, but subsequent decades of management experience had included the Irish singer Chris Doran, who went to number one in the United States. Julian now placed ads in *The Stage Online, Star Now*, the BRIT School and other performance academies, inviting hopefuls to send in audition videos. "We had about 300 people interested," he says. "We eventually whittled it down to 20 hopefuls. We got them to sing, put the guys together in different formations, had them as a five-piece and then re-auditioned them."

The timing was right. One Direction were about to burst on to the scene; The Wanted were doing well and Take That had just proved that it was entirely possible not only to make a pro-longed career as a boy band but to maintain the status of heart-throbs well into their forties. Not that manufactured boy bands were anything new – just look at The Monkees, way back in the sixties. And if you got the formula right, the rewards were significant for everyone involved.

Julian White had recently negotiated a big publishing deal for The Look with Demon Music Group, as well as managing Dale Saunders and working with Flo Rida. Soon to collaborate with will.i.am in 2013, it's clear he was then the right man for the job.

Julian had managed Kasey Monroe, a songwriter from Edinburgh, to whom he had been introduced by a pre-fame Simon Cowell in the days when he ran Fanfare Records. Kasey had many years' experience in the business, had moved into management and now had a proven track record of discovering new talent. Having started off playing in various bands, she now owned her own recording studios and would later sign song-writing deals with Virgin, EMI and BMG. Now in partnership with multi-platinum producer Ian Curnow, Kasey had discovered new faces including Heidi Range of Sugababes. Dividing her time between London and Los Angeles, she'd also had a huge success with Kumi Koda, one of the biggest Japanese stars of the day, via a collaboration negotiated by Julian White.

Kasey Monroe was also keen on putting together a new boy band, partly as a vehicle for her own songs. Given that she had worked with the producers of One Direction and Girls Aloud, she was in an ideal position to do so. With Ian Curnow as the third music biz veteran on the project, the hunt was on.

Kasey handled the day-to-day viewing of audition videos. She got her shortlist to perform an original song she had written, on the grounds that it's more difficult to perform an original than a cover version; she also invited a young man she had seen perform in a band called Boulevard to join the new group, when the other members had finally been chosen. His name was Josh Cuthbert and, had Kasey not pursued him to join, Union J would not exist in its current format. The other two 'J's had sent in audition tapes, but Josh, who was at that stage heartily disillusioned with the music industry, did not. However, Kasey had a very experienced eye and knew a star in the making when she saw one.

The group began to take shape. The initial line-up of five was Josh, JJ, Jaymi, Billy Humphreys and a boy named Mark. But when Julian saw the completed line-up, he wasn't happy with Mark. After a further range of auditions was held, Ben Weeden joined the band instead. (Ben is still singing with a band called Base, while Billy has left the industry.)

After some thought, Kasey decided to call the new outfit Rewind (of which more later). She, Julian and Ian started getting the band into shape, at a point when they were all holding down other jobs as well: JJ was still involved with horses and worked in stable yards, although by now he'd had experience of other bands, and Josh was working for a computer company. Josh was based in Camberley, Surrey, but the other two members of what is now Union J were commuting from their parents' homes in Newmarket and Luton. At that stage, no one wanted to risk giving up their full-time occupations for what was still a very uncertain future – they'd all had some experience of the industry by now, and knew how fickle it could be.

Julian remembers them well. "Josh wanted to be the leader of the band," he says. "We gave him that early on, but to be honest, the power went to his head. He could be a funny guy, but also overbearing. In a way, he tried too hard to be nice. JJ is a really nice guy, quiet and shy. He had been in bands since leaving the racing world and when he joined Rewind, he naturally moved over from that world into this one. He was honest and likeable and showed none of the bitchiness you sometimes get in boy bands. It was the biggest shame about his going. Jaymi – initially I liked him. He was very flamboyant and funny and looked good. But he was not always very kind."

At the time, Jaymi was already in a relationship with Olly, his long-term partner, Josh was dating Chess Jones, while sharing a flat with her brother, and JJ was, in Julian's words, a serial dater with a girlfriend in every town. And why not? They were young men, enjoying themselves, although the only relationship to survive from that particular period would be that of Jaymi and Olly.

Julian recalls how, on another occasion, he took Jaymi to the famous gay nightclub Heaven, where everyone had a riotous time. "We had a lot of trouble styling Jaymi as he was going bald and we had to use a hair piece," he rather wickedly recollects. "It was funny, watching *The X Factor*, as the hair piece grew on a weekly basis!" Jaymi also had a lot of tattoos that had to be covered up, although his bandmates would do their best to catch up with him.

Kasey remembers them slightly differently. "JJ didn't have a clue – he wasn't a singer," she says. "He'd tried to be in bands previously, but he was still working in stables. However, he was very likeable, easy to get on with and keen. And he wanted to be famous. Josh was an absolute star. As soon as I saw him, I thought, 'He has the look.' He was a good singer, but he was also very lazy, on top of which his girlfriend, Chess, didn't want him to be rehearsing with us, but to spend time with her."

Josh at that stage was not particularly bothered about whether or not they would make it: he was a young man having fun and he'd already had a few bad experiences in show business, which were putting him off. His relationship dominated his life at that stage, which didn't help when it came to turning up to rehearsals or putting the time in.

"She was always making plans for them – they used to fight all the time," Kasey remembers. "Josh didn't have a lot of ambition at this point: he'd been in bands before and people had promised him things which didn't materialise and he'd pretty much given up. He'd been in another band that got signed to a major label, but they were then dropped – he was pretty messed around and had all but given up the music business. Sometimes we wanted to sack him because he didn't turn up, but he was a talented singer. He hated dancing."

Kasey is a little more cautious on the subject of Jaymi. "Jaymi was a diva," she says flatly. "He's got a good singing voice, but he'd been to stage school and had a bit of an attitude." Jaymi had been to the Sylvia Young school in London, as had Josh, but, contrary to other reports, the two hadn't known one another at the time and met for the first time when introduced by Kasey. Jaymi and Billy had been in a band together before and so were already acquainted, which would have a bearing on what happened when Rewind split up and turned into Triple J.

In the early days of Rewind, however, the boys formed particular friendships within the band. JJ and Josh became firm friends, as did Jaymi and Billy. When Ben joined, he took up with JJ and Josh. There was some rivalry between Jaymi and Josh initially, with the odd quarrel about who would wear or sing what, but everyone rubbed along together OK. They would rehearse in a dance studio in Camberley where Doris Pearson, who had once been a member of the group Five Star, worked to get them into shape, as well as at Julian's house. The meetings could be sporadic, with the boys complaining that they were ready to get out there and didn't need to rehearse.

Julian disagreed. "The guys spent the majority of their time with us in London staying at mine or each other's homes," he recalls. "We had vocal lessons as at first JJ wasn't a great singer until we turned that around. We had choreographed them with Doris Pearson from Five Star as they had two left feet, so we heavily rehearsed and had a studio booked and a big writer from Germany coming over."

In the meantime, Josh and Ben had developed a really close friendship, hanging out with each other a lot. It would make subsequent events particularly difficult for them.

Whatever tensions and rivalries might have existed, it was becoming apparent that Rewind were turning into an outfit that had a serious future ahead of them. Under the guidance of Ms Pearson, they were learning to harmonise properly, learning stagecraft and how to react to one another, how to move and how to sing. They looked the part, which is crucial for the success of any boy band; although sometimes reluctant to rehearse, they were together enough to show serious promise.

Julian White began thinking about which of his contacts in the music industry to introduce the band to at this point, spreading the word that a major new talent had appeared on the scene. A buzz began to build around them – although this would actually create the circumstances that snatched them away to work with someone else. But at the time, all anyone thought was that the boys showed extreme promise·and, with a lot more hard work, could well have a serious future ahead of them. Everything was positive as long as the boys worked at their act.

Everyone had been working together for the best part of a year when Julian asked them to sign a Heads of Agreement – a non-binding precursor to a proper management contract. Having put considerable time and effort into training the boys, he was understandably keen to get everything in writing with formal contracts and start the work properly. He went to an entertainment lawyer, Alexis Grower at McGrath & Co, to get everything finalised. But it would not work out as planned.

As long as no formal contract had been signed, the boys were pretty much free to do what they wanted. By now they had turned into a highly promising five-piece outfit with ideas of their own about where they wanted to head next. And that was to *The X Factor.*

While the boys dilly-dallied about committing themselves to working with Julian, Kasey and Ian, private discussions were going on in the background and the formal contract remained unsigned. Then, one afternoon that summer, matters came to a head. First, Julian got an email from JJ saying that he was leaving the band. This was followed by another one from Josh an hour later, saying the same thing, and finally one from Jaymi. Rewind, in that particular formation, was no more. It didn't take long before Julian found out why.

"I heard on the grapevine Blair [Dreelan] coaxed them over," he says. "I was peed off – it had been a year's work and effort all at my expense. I was really annoyed and Jaymi got quite aggressive with me on the phone."

At one point the possibility of legal action against Dreelan was mooted – but in the event the idea would be dropped, when he too was dropped by the boys as their manager. The overriding problem was that no formal management contract had ever been signed. Not a lot could be done about it, but in the longer term Kasey would come to feel the biggest injustice was that they had somehow been whitewashed from the band's history. They had never known George Shelley, of course, but they were there at the beginning of what is now Union J.

Initially, Kasey had never heard of Blair Dreelan; but he'd had dealings with Josh years earlier, and so became aware that his old friend was in a new band when photos of the boys went up on Facebook. Julian had also sent demos the boys had made to Chris Herbert, a talent manager who'd dealt with The Spice Girls in the past. Herbert apparently mentioned that he thought the new group was good, and so Blair set out to track them down.

(Despite my attempts to contact him, Blair Dreelan did not respond to my requests for an interview. The following is there-fore inevitably coloured by how Kasey Monroe and Julian White saw it.)

Dreelan approached three of the boys, say Monroe and White, with a proposal to get them onto *The X Factor*. He targeted JJ, Josh and Jaymi because they were dark-haired and told the other two, who were blonder, that if they dyed their hair they could come too; they declined. Josh, however, did not want to leave the current set-up, not least because of his friend-ship with Ben, and he was very unhappy about his loyalties being torn in two different directions.

Ultimately, however, the opportunity was just too good to miss, and so the bombshell was dropped. The three of them were off; what had seemed a very promising set-up as Rewind had changed into the form of Triple J.

(It clearly worked, though it would be far from perfect – in that a threesome is very different from a quintet. *The X Factor* bosses saw that too, which is why George is now part of the band.)

"If the boys had wanted to do *X Factor*, we'd have let them," says Kasey, with some sadness. It was not a happy parting – there was a terrible altercation on the telephone with Jaymi and lingering bitterness about the way matters had turned out. Apart from anything else, the songwriter from Germany was due to come over.

"When they walked out this left a big expense as flights were booked and the studio booked," says Julian. "They really let a lot of people down which was a great shame, as I believed they didn't need *X Factor* to get a deal as they had developed into a great five piece with tight harmonies. Now as a four they're carried alone by Jaymi – who I believe will go solo in the end, dropping the other three."

At the moment, of course, there is no sign of that – the boys clearly feel the act works as a foursome, although who knows what the future will bring?

But at the time it was all rather messy. The two boys that had been left behind were pretty gutted as well. "The other two were devastated as I had lined up meetings with Universal that looked very promising," Julian recalls. "Billy gave up altogether and Ben formed another band which didn't work out."

Of course, with Ben it wasn't just a professional blow – his friendship with Josh was bound to suffer, something that both found very upsetting. But now there was no turning back. The die was cast, the boys had made their decision and it was time to get on with the new act.

"Ben was gutted when he heard," says Kasey. "And Jaymi had spoken to Billy about doing *The X Factor* together, so he didn't believe it at first. I personally felt gutted and felt for the other guys, too. By this time we'd heard the rumours that Blair was after them, but Josh had no time for Blair. I couldn't believe it."

But it was done – the boys had changed management and soon renamed themselves Triple J. Julian only found out that they were planning to appear on *The X Factor* when a contact in the music business saw them in the studios and phoned up with the news. But by then a new chapter had started in everyone's lives.

It must be said that the picture Blair Dreelan painted was very different from this. Also known as 'Sparx', he grew up in Dedworth, Windsor and studied at the East Berks Langley performing arts school. Blair worked with Lemar, Liberty X, Peter André, Westlife and quite a few other acts before turning his hand to songwriting. Working with Ray Hedges of Mothership Productions, he signed a publishing deal with Bucks Music and went on to found his own production team. A working partnership with East 17 followed that, and Blair also had a prior association with *The X Factor*, having been picked out at auditions three times with his band 4th Ba5e. Rather more unfortunately, he lost his dancer girlfriend, Sarah Robinson, to Matt Cardle during the 11th series of the show, which garnered a huge amount of publicity at the time.

On one such previous occasion, in 2007, he met Josh, who was auditioning for *The X Factor* as a soloist. Neither was successful, but they joined a boyband called M4, which would disband in 2009. They stayed vaguely in touch, which is what brought matters to a head after the boys had spent a year with Julian White. Blair Dreelan heard about this new act, realised he knew one of the members and decided to act.

It is not something Blair has talked about much, preferring to concentrate on what he sees as the more positive aspects of the story. "Basically I met the boys over a period of time," he told sugarscape.com as they started to gather a huge following on *The X Factor* and interest was growing massively. As he explained it, his history with Josh went back a few years. "I actually met Josh Cuthbert when he was 14 and he was auditioning as a solo artist on *The X Factor*. I literally just spotted him when I was walking through the crowd and I thought he had a really good look about him, he looked like a pop star. I stopped him and he was with his mum and I asked if I could hear him sing, he sang and I thought he had a great voice. I began to sort of work with him on various little projects, like just sort of recording stuff because I've got a recording studio in Swindon. Josh kind of became almost a bit like my little brother you know, as he got older he started to come out with me at the weekends and stuff."

The meeting with JJ had been totally different, occurring very much by accident. "And then JJ Hamblett I actually met in a hotel reception, we had a mutual friend and we just started talking," Blair continued. "I said to him about singing and stuff and got his details. I really liked the way JJ looked, I thought he had – do you remember that TV show in the nineties, *Saved By The Bell* and stuff like that? He reminded me of – not his actual look, but the way he is – of Johnny Depp when he was in a TV series called *21 Jump Street*. That was the series that actually launched Johnny Depp and made him like a teenage heart-throb. In my head he had a nineties teenage heart-throb look. Jaymi Hensley and Josh went to Sylvia Young Theatre School just for weekend classes on a Saturday so [they] knew each other from there, and then obviously George was a solo act on *The X Factor*, so I met George through the show."

But the overriding factor for all of them was that they possessed star quality. They radiated charisma, something that all the rehearsals in the world won't create for you. Union J's members would probably have made it on their own whatever the conditions, but the four of them together exploded with energy, talent and ambition. Even Josh, so disheartened by his previous experiences, was beginning to realise what possibilities awaited him, his star quality outweighing his disillusionment. All four of them were about to come into their own.

What was done was done. The music business is a cutthroat

arena, and it certainly wasn't the first time that an act put together by one manager had defected to another on the verge of making it big. (Something similar had happened in the early days of the Spice Girls.) Whatever the rights and wrongs, the band was poised to step on to greater things. The missing factor would later manifest in the shape of George Shelley, and it wasn't long before he too came onboard.

"When they suggested it, it made sense as we'd even spotted George at Boot Camp and asked him to sing for us," said Josh to *We Love Pop* magazine. "The rest of us had only known each other for about a month [sic] when Jaymi applied for *The X Factor*. So when George came along it wasn't a big deal, as we were literally all so new to each other anyway."

They were certainly new to what was happening to them now, although it remained a gamble: Triple J didn't make it through in that particular set-up and were lucky to have been rescued at the last minute, but they were now on a roll. They had everything to play for and they were about to become the focus of the nation's prime-time television viewing. They were young, they were ready to go for it and nothing could stop them now.

Julian White, Kasey Monroe and Ian Curnow remain as active in the music world as ever; although saddened by the way things turned out, they have moved on. Kasey, in particular, has gone on to manage a new version of Rewind, comprising Lewis Irons, Andy Bargh, Ryan Donaldson, James McElvar and Jack Robertson. So far there are no plans to put them on *The X Factor* – but there again, a week can be a very long time in the world of pop.

3

Behind The Scenes At The Auditions

April 2012.

The show business world was abuzz. Always full of rumour, gossip and speculation, the focus now was on the ninth series of *The X Factor*, the reality television show that had turned the world of music upside down. Once upon a time, becoming a star had involved years of hard slog to build up a following and tours consisted of the smallest, least prestigious gigs in the land. But these days, the best way to launch a musical career was on the back of a reality TV show, particularly if it involved the extraordinary impresario Simon Cowell.

Reality shows didn't get any bigger than *The X Factor*. Although it was only on television screens for two months at a time, it was a constant topic of conversation throughout the rest of the year as well.

This particular year, there had already been a huge amount of interest in a biography of Cowell by the writer Tom Bower, which revealed amongst other things his affair with Dannii Minogue. It all served to keep interest in the show up to boiling point.

The X Factor harked back to the glory days of British television, when a nation gathered to watch a particular programme and then regrouped around the water cooler to talk about it at work. It also echoed another staple of British entertainment: a variety show, a format so beloved of the public that there was even a Royal Variety Show, when the Windsors got to watch a proliferation of acts along with their subjects.

Broadcast to the nation as a competition, *The X Factor* was not just a talent showcase but a chance to pitch people from obscurity to international stardom. The stakes were huge, the whole country got behind individual contestants and the excitement was palpable, both onscreen and off.

Simon Cowell, one of the canniest men in show business, was well aware that drama exacerbated interest in the show. He had not officially cooperated on the biography – and indeed, its representation of him as less than gallant in his dealings with women had invited a minor backlash – but he knew more than anyone that all publicity was good publicity and constant snippets of information only served to heighten interest. It all fed directly back into the Cowell coffers when Syco, his record label, signed the most promising contestants; if their careers took off, all well and good, and if they didn't – well, there was always another show. But the release of information was certainly not confined to Cowell's personal life. It also involved gossip and speculation about spats among the judges, and in spring 2012 it was business as usual on that front.

For a start, Cowell and fellow judge Cheryl Cole – according to Bower's book, a lust object for Cowell – had a spectacular bust-up in the US version of the show, which had been widely reported back in the UK and served, as always, to sharpen public interest in what was going on behind the scenes. Then there was the usual speculation about who was to appear as a judge on the show that year – Cowell, ever mischievous, had publicly announced that he would like Jessie J, then presenting *The Voice* on BBC1, as a judge on *The X Factor*. Jessie was publicly obliged to turn it down, and in another Cowell-engineered twist of events, *The X Factor* and *The Voice* were set up in the public eye as rivals, with all of the enjoyable feuding it entailed.

The first *X Factor* judge to be confirmed was the enormously popular Gary Barlow, who had proven a very popular choice the previous year and had taken Marcus Collins to the live finale at Wembley Arena. "I'm thrilled to be back and really looking forward to working with *The X Factor* team again," he told ITV. "The fact that a superstar could just walk out on that stage is very exciting."

And who better than Barlow to judge who it might be? Although a highly talented musician who'd worked with some of the biggest names in the business in his own right, Gary was also a member of Take That, one of the most successful boybands that ever existed. He knew just how well a manufactured boyband could work, and this was reflected in his fee for judging the competition – a cool £2 million.

Next up was Louis Walsh, who had been with the show since its inception in 2004. He lost no time in trashing the competition, albeit by citing another programme as the yardstick: "I'm so glad that *Britain's Got Talent* is beating *The Voice*," he told *Heat* magazine. "I think everyone thought *The Voice UK* would be like the US version, and it's not. It's dull and boring. I'm glad *BGT* is winning the ratings battle – it's much better."

If that were not enough, he revealed there was "no love lost" between Cowell and *The Voice* presenter will.i.am. "What's that man's real name anyway? It's not will.i.am, is it?" Walsh inquired. "The way he dresses at his age . . . what's that silly glove all about? He thinks he's got all the answers, but if he didn't have Fergie in that band [the Black Eyed Peas], where would he be? Fergie is the real star. I would love her on *The X Factor*, and to be a judge on the show." But would he want to leave *The X Factor* for *The Voice*? "No way, it's not great TV – it's like *Fame Academy* all those years ago," came the unsurprising reply.

Jessie J took the bait and responded in kind: "I think you should always be respectful of other people who have had success and had a career. And yeah, I don't know how I'd feel taking vocal advice from someone who doesn't sing, but Louis Walsh, you're a nice guy. Just keep it nice," she told Capital Radio.

All the same, the point had been made and everyone was happy that it kept *The X Factor* in the public eye. A contestant who had been on both shows spoke up for *The Voice*, saying it had treated her with more respect, but once again, all the controversy did was to whet more appetites for what was to come next. Louis Walsh, who appeared to be relishing the spats, then took aim at previous judge Cheryl Cole, after the Girls Aloud singer claimed in an interview with *Marie Claire* that Louis had "zero involvement" with her band while he was their manager. "Our friendship is over," spat Louis in *The Sun*. The public lapped it up.

Drip by drip, news about the line-up of the other judges began to appear. Tulisa Contostavlos, who had been on the previous series, was to reappear, and it didn't hurt matters one jot that the timing of the announcement came hot on the heels of the release of a sex tape involving her and her previous boyfriend, Justin Edwards. Cowell publicly reassured her that it would not affect her return to *The X Factor* and that he was "100 per cent" behind her.

Tulisa also got a pay rise – a fee of £500,000, up from £200,000 the previous year, and was responsible for generating a huge amount of publicity via interviews on her feelings about that sex tape and becoming a judge on *The X Factor*. The publicity machine rolled on and it didn't hurt when an *FHM* poll named her as the sexiest woman in the world. Shortly after this, Tulisa's single, 'Young', went to number one – a classic example of one publicity machine feeding another, with mutually beneficial results for all.

The only exception to the rule that all publicity was good publicity was Louis Walsh. The previous year, dance teacher Leonard Watters had claimed Louis groped him in an upmarket Dublin club, a story that was totally untrue and for which Watters ended up in jail. It had affected Walsh badly, however, and there was now a certain wariness that led him to avoid public situations far more than previously, spending his time primarily in the company of close friends. But still, *The X Factor* brought out the best in him and the old Louis, the gossiping music man, returned to the fore once more. Back in his familiar territory, he would play a particularly pivotal role in the show.

Simon Cowell was not actually going to be present on the show, as he was busy with the US version at the time (although his presence continued to dominate all the rumours and negotiations, the gossip and the fallouts), and so a fourth judge was required. The most obvious choice was Kelly Rowland, who had been on the previous series, but she turned it down on the grounds of too many other commitments.

(There were also rumours that she was not totally happy with the remuneration she had been offered for the show, having requested £1.5 million and been turned down. The previous year she had been paid £500,000 and it seemed the producers did not want to go higher than that.)

There were rumoured approaches to Sharon Osbourne and Dannii Minogue, both past judges, as well as Katy Perry and Rihanna, all of whom turned it down. The rows over Cowell's biography showed no sign of dying down and it was perhaps unsurprising that Dannii, whose fling with him had been exposed, was said to be massively embarrassed and in no mood to appear on the show, despite offers reported to be worth £1 million. Reports claimed that a smarting Dannii refused to do it for less than £5 million – which was not forthcoming.

There was by this time a real sense of panic building behind the scenes: while there were plenty of entertainers who'd be only too happy to join the judging panel and revel in the attention, none of them was deemed to be quite right. It was a tricky business being a judge, because a certain personality was called for that had the ability to be caustic and sympathetic all at once.

So who would it be? And would they actually manage to find someone before the contest began?

Louis Walsh added fuel to the fire by publicly saying that not only did he want Sharon to return, he also felt Tulisa should be axed in her favour. This was, of course, another carefully calculated move: when the show got underway, the judges would be competing with each other as much as the actual contestants were. It did no harm to sow a little discord before proceedings even began. A sense of tension between the judges added to the drama of the show, something of which every participant was aware.

Cowell had also offered Cheryl Cole the opportunity to return to the UK version of the show after the debacle in the

US, but she too was still smarting, from what she perceived as his betrayal of her in the States. A war of words broke out between the two of them, with Tom Bower, author of the Cowell biography, chipping in to say he hadn't found her particularly intelligent. But while all this generated acres of publicity, it still didn't answer the big question – who was going to be the fourth judge on the show? Gary had an idea of his own: he tweeted that eighties pop star Boy George would make a good judge, but George wasn't signed either.

By this time the audition stage was approaching and still no permanent replacement had been found. The rumour mill went into overdrive, but eventually it was announced that there would be a series of guest judges including Geri Halliwell, Leona Lewis (who had won the third series of the show), Rita Ora, Nicole Scherzinger, Mel B and Anastacia. In the longer term, Nicole was to fill the role of fourth judge on a permanent basis from the Newcastle auditions onwards.

The judges were expected to sing for their supper, of course, as Louis (who had known Cowell for 20 years and was very close to him behind the scenes) made clear. "Everyone has to up their game this year," he told the *Daily Mirror*. "Tulisa has to work harder and Gary has to be more fun. He has to chill out. He was too serious last year." The judges took it to heart.

Otherwise the lineup was the same. Dermot O'Leary was to present the main show on ITV – he managed to generate some publicity for calling on the show's producers to take the auditions back to his native Ireland, a routine they had scrapped two years previously – while Caroline Flack and Olly Murs were to present *The Xtra Factor*, the back-up show on ITV2. That was the theory, at any rate – in reality, Olly was away for the auditions, 'Boot Camp' and 'Judges' Houses' segments as he was on tour. Instead, his place was taken by a series of guests including Jedward, JLS and Westlife.

While Cowell may not have been appearing on the show himself, he continued to take a very close interest in the proceedings. *The Voice* was losing viewers hand over fist and, while Simon couldn't resist poking fun at the programme, he also expressed some relief that it had not proven to be the major rival some people had feared. "That show puzzles me because it starts off and 'it's all about the voice,'" he told James Naughtie on Radio 4's *Today* programme. "So my first thought is, 'Why isn't this on radio?' because what's the point in looking at them. Then suddenly I'm watching it a week or two weeks ago and it's the same as *The X Factor*. They've got dancers behind them, graphics, lights. Same show. I see a lot of shows trying to rip us off. If you try and rip somebody off it always looks like a bad copy. You've got to find a different way of doing things."

Cowell also revealed his delight that One Direction, who had appeared in a previous series, were doing so well, having turned into globally feted megastars. It was a classic case of *The X Factor* doing what it was supposed to do: turning ordinary people into megastars and perpetuating its own future as a television show. If it didn't produce the stars, then there was no point in it continuing to exist.

This year though, the selection process for competitors was a little different. Cowell was well aware of the need for constant innovation and his shows were not to be allowed to atrophy. For the first time ever, potential acts were invited to post video performances on the Facebook audition tab of the show's page. Another innovation was that singers or groups were now allowed to apply even if they already had a management deal (or had one in the past). Indeed, there had been rumours about previous contestants with managers in earlier episodes of the show and it merely served to remove a potential embarrassment if they surfaced again.

It also benefited the boys who were to become Union J, as they had already attracted the attentions of not one but two managers. There was concern that it might give some contestants an unfair advantage, but producer Richard Holloway denied this: "Everybody that comes along and applies to the show all goes through the same process. Every single person, whether they have got any form of management or not . . ."

Tulisa also gave the move her backing. "There are so many people out there that are so talented, who have managers," she said to the *Metro* newspaper. "Just because they have a manager doesn't mean it's easier for them to make it than anybody else. I think it's just about being fair. It's a stigma that if you've had experience you shouldn't be allowed on the show. I think it's a load of rubbish."

The new ruling reflected the reality – that as the show was increasingly seen as the way to make it professionally, many ambitious singers and groups were bound to have someone already representing them at hand.

A further innovation was to introduce 'van auditions' – the show sent a mobile audition van to 18 cities across the country, on the grounds that not everyone would be able to make the big arena auditions. It was a way of getting an increasing number of people involved in the show, and a team of researchers was sent out to invite particular people to appear. Although there was a slight outcry when this latter point came to light, it had in fact been in the online terms and conditions from the start:

> Please note that outside of this application process, acts
> may also be invited to audition for the programme by

researchers acting on behalf of the producer. Such acts will be required to go through the audition process and normal programme rules will apply.

The reason for all of this was the same: there were concerns about flagging ratings and the producers wanted to find the best talent available. It was all to strengthen the show's appeal, not to introduce any unfair advantages. In yet another innovation, the acts were also allowed to play their own instruments and compositions right from the start, something that had only ever been allowed (with various restrictions) on the live shows in the past.

There was certainly a sense that *The X Factor* needed a shake-up. The success of One Direction aside, the previous series had been somewhat lacklustre and serious efforts were going on backstage to give the show some added verve. Gary Barlow defended the move to invite specific contestants to audition, saying it would make the amateurs up their game; he also revealed how Cowell was taking a very close interest in proceedings. "We had a big review with Simon about the show and the acts," Gary said in an interview with *The Sun*. "His thing with me is that he never talks about what you say as a judge, he's always about the acts. He says we've got to find more stars, we've got to develop them, we've got to look back at the tapes from last year and see if there are people we've missed. It's always about the talent and that's the same reason I'm here, finding talent." He was going to succeed.

Cowell's overwhelming influence (and why not – after all, it is *his* show) also came out in an interview with Dermot O'Leary. "Everything and nothing surprises me about Simon – he's very enigmatic," Dermot told *The Sun*. "You can speak to him for five days a week, then you won't hear from him for a couple of months. Quite often I'd go into his dressing room and he'd be having a bath. He's always having baths at the most inappropriate time of day. Even lunchtime. But he's the boss. He's open to suggestions, though. I once gave him a list of songs that I thought would work well for Boot Camp and some got included. He's a meritocrat. He wants people to succeed at their job and he likes people to show a bit of balls and not be too safe."

Cowell was particularly open to suggestions that involved mixing it up and playing to the unexpected – one example being taking a group of three young male contestants, adding a solo act and creating a new group in front of the entire nation. Louis (or possibly Caroline) and the others on *The X Factor* might have come up with the idea of Union J, but in doing so they were well aware that Cowell would be delighted. It was the kind of edgy television he wanted, and the icing on the cake was that it would discover people who were going to become major stars. It was what *The X Factor* was there to do and, in this case, it succeeded brilliantly. Everyone turned out to be a winner – although it wouldn't be evident for some months yet.

Originally, the judges' auditions had been due to start on May 15, 2012, but because of the ongoing search for a fourth judge they were postponed until May 23. The first audition was held at the Liverpool Echo Arena, before moving on to London, Manchester, Glasgow, Newcastle and Cardiff. Geri Halliwell was guest judge on the first audition in Liverpool; as a big name her presence was a relief to the producers, who had still not settled on a permanent appointment. Geri good-naturedly played the game, saying that if she was there during the 'Judges' Houses' stage, she'd "possibly ask George" (Michael) for assistance and that, if she were still a young wannabe, she'd audition for the show herself.

For the first audition in Liverpool, all the judges made a huge effort to make a big entrance – none more so than Geri. Arriving in a tight blue lace mini-dress and grey ankle boots, she climbed on to the top of her limousine and began greeting the crowds through a loudhailer. Her nan was from Liverpool, she told the assembled crowd, before adding, perhaps unwisely: "Between me and Gary, we've had 22 number ones! That's as much as The Beatles!" The assembled crowd looked less than impressed and, amidst the cheering, the odd boo could also be heard.

No matter: the ninth series of *The X Factor* was about to begin. Geri redeemed herself by climbing off the limo and going off to glad-hand the crowd, as the other judges turned up: Tulisa in a short floral number set off by a huge studded belt and red platform shoes, Gary opting for a simple black jacket over white T-shirt with black stripes, and Louis casual in light grey shirt and dark grey jacket. Dermot O'Leary and Caroline Flack were also in attendance to join the fun.

Of course, it would be months before anything actually appeared on television, but the juggernaut that was Britain's most successful talent contest-cum-reality show was under way. Everyone knew what was at stake (including the future of the programme – it was imperative that they find a big star), but the old pros began talking it up as never before. Louis Walsh, in particular, knew what had to be done and that the winner was not necessarily going to be the one who turned into a big star.

"Look at One Direction, nobody predicted how big they'd be," he told the *Daily Mirror*. "JLS, Olly Murs, Rebecca Ferguson. None of them won the show. Personally I'd love to find a great male singer – a young Tom Jones, or an English Michael Bublé. There is a huge gap there."

In actual fact, a very different set of superstars were set to appear. Tense, nervous, but also hugely excited, the four future members of Union J were about to get caught up in the biggest talent show of all time.

4

On With The Show

The judges' auditions had taken place in May 2012, but it was not until August that the series began to air and the rest of the country was given a look at them. At first, nothing very remarkable came to light. The first auditions that aired were filmed in London and Manchester, with Nicole Scherzinger acting as the stand-in judge in London – she had still not been confirmed as the permanent fourth judge when filming took place – and Mel B in Manchester. The very first act to appear was a 17-year-old singer called Sheyi, a Nando's worker who, sadly, failed to impress and didn't get through.

Next up was a Pink tribute act called Zoe Alexander, who looked, sounded and dressed like Pink, sang a Pink number and then informed the judges she wanted to be "myself". She didn't get through either, although she certainly proved to be a memorable candidate. First she tried to smash some of the onstage equipment after arguing with the judges about her number, Pink's 'So What', insisting she had been forced to sing it. Gary asked her to sing 'Next To Me' by Emeli Sandé: when that went down badly, she threw her microphone down and stormed offstage. Her father brought her back on, where she distinguished herself by swearing at the judges, first hitting a camera operator and then a female producer, and ending up being cautioned by the police.

The incident caused such a controversy that executive producer Richard Holloway was forced to make a statement:

> All the contestants that go in front of the judges, they're all spoken to by the production team as they have to get all the tracks to play, so the conversation takes place between them and us about what they want to sing, they go through their choices and the final decision about what they are going to sing when they walk on the stage is theirs, 100 per cent theirs.

It certainly provided the show with a talking point.

There followed Jahmene Douglas, another solo performer, the first of the night to make it through to the next round. Then it was over to Manchester, where Mel B told an 82-year-old singer called Gary he was putting her to sleep ("Heartless," said Dermot), before Curtis Golden and Ella Henderson were also put through to the next stage. So far, so unremarkable.

And so it went on. Right from the start, as ever, everyone was looking out for the person or persons who would turn out to have that certain indefinable *it*, but the names that surfaced in those early days were not the ones who came to dominate proceedings. There was Lucy Spraggan, who was already creating something of a stir with her self-released single, 'Last Night', which she performed at her audition and which entered the charts at number 11 after it was broadcast. (It was later taken off iTunes at the request of *The X Factor*'s producers.)

There was Britt Love from the pop duo Mini Viva, who initially made a big impression on the judges. As half of the duo with Frankee Connolly, she'd had a Top 10 single with 'Left My

Heart In Tokyo', and toured with The Saturdays and Girls Aloud. However, further success had failed to materialise, which is why she'd ended up on the show – as one of the new class of contestants who wouldn't have been allowed on previously – and got an enthusiastic response from all four judges, who put her through.

There was also Bianca Gascoigne, Paul Gascoigne's step-daughter, TV presenter and actress Hayley Evetts, who had previously been on *Popstars* and *Pop Idol*, Stephanie McMichael, who had been in *Big Brother 9* and in the group Poisonous Twin, and Nathan Fagan-Gayle, who had appeared on *Celebrity Hijack*. In addition to all of these, there was Joe Cox, Jade Richards, Melanie McCabe and Carolynne Poole, all of whom had been on the show in series eight and all of whom had reached the 'Judges' Houses' stage. These were the people attracting attention early on – not the ones who were actually going to become big stars.

The next stage in the competition was Boot Camp. For the first time ever it was held outside London (as the capital was hosting the 2012 Olympics), taking place at the Echo Arena in Liverpool over the course of three days in July. A hugely enthusiastic crowd turned out to greet the judges. The first to arrive was Nicole Scherzinger, now a permanent fixture on the show, wearing silver spray-on jeans, a printed T-shirt and black waistcoat; following her came a beaming Gary Barlow, clad in fawn chinos and a grey top, Louis and Tulisa, with newly bleached-blonde hair in a side plait, leather shorts and an animal print bomber jacket. Caroline Flack and Kian Egan were also present to help kick things off with a launch at the trendy Alma de Cuba, a former church that had been turned into a restaurant and bar. JLS were the series' first high-profile guest stars, performing

'Everybody In Love' in the bar area which had been converted into a studio. Spirits were high.

The stakes were, too. It was at this stage that things actually began to get serious, as the wheat was separated from the chaff. A whopping 211 acts reached Boot Camp, but the judges eliminated 60 of them on the basis of the audition tapes alone before they'd even had a chance to sing. The remaining contestants were, as usual, separated into four categories: boys, girls, groups and over-28s.

(The last category had originally been over-25s, but Cowell was trying his hardest to bring in as much real talent as he could, believing that the previous series had suffered as many of the contestants were just a little too young. The boys and girls categories would therefore include contestants between the ages of 16 and 27, something that had worked with some success in the seventh series of the show.)

Everyone who was left now had a choice of songs to perform: 'Stronger (What Doesn't Kill You)', 'Respect', 'Moves Like Jagger', 'Are You Gonna Go My Way', 'Crazy In Love', 'Next To Me', 'She Said', 'Use Somebody' and 'How To Save A Life'. Now the number of acts was reduced still further down to 70, comprising 21 girls, 22 boys, 12 over-28s and 15 groups. There was still all to play for – apart from those mentioned above, no one as yet had really stood out. This though was about to change.

The following day, each act performed for the judges in front of a live audience. On the day after that came the big moment when the judges decided who would go through to the Judges' Houses. This is when it started to get really interesting: the judges were intrigued by two groups, Triple J and GMD3, but couldn't decide between them and so made each one perform again. In the end it was GMD3 who made it – and Triple J were sent home.

Tensions were beginning to rise. Everyone left in the competition was aware that they now had a real chance to change their lives. As if to mark the occasion, Simon Cowell put in a personal appearance, his first since leaving at the end of the seventh series. As he was in Miami, working on the US series of the show, his message had to be delivered by phone. Much in the manner of a Bond villain (or Charlie of *Charlie's Angels*), he phoned through his instructions to the judges: Nicole was to mentor the boys out in Dubai, helped by R&B star Ne-Yo; Tulisa was off to St Lucia to mentor the girls, ably assisted by Tinie Tempah; Louis was off to Las Vegas with the groups, in the company of Sharon Osbourne. Gary, originally due to fly to Majorca, opted to stay in the UK, where he was based at Boughton House in Northamptonshire; his wife, Dawn, had only recently suffered a tragic stillbirth.

He was to be assisted with the over-28s by Cheryl Cole, whose involvement was shrouded in great secrecy: when she made her surprise arrival in the grounds of the house as the contest heated up, not only did the contestants have their phones removed, but she was hidden under a tablecloth so no one could see her sitting next to Gary. She had arrived in some style, in a helicopter, and beamed at the clearly stunned contestants: "I've been in both positions, I've been here and I've been on your side, so I know how you are feeling," she said. "I'm just so excited to be here. I wish you all the best of luck." It was a sensational development and quite a coup for Simon – clearly, relations between the two of them were nothing like as bad as had been implied.

It was at this stage that the dramatic turnaround occurred:

Triple J, having believed they were out of the contest, learned that they were very much back in it again with a new, additional member. The gloves were off; this was going to be the fight of their lives.

And so the next phase of the programme began. The media attention, never lax at the best of times, stepped up a notch. Tinie Tempah told the *Daily Mirror* he was advising the girls to get their heads down and work hard. "This experience could change their life − it's not worth ruining it for a night out," he said. "Maybe this is going to make me sound like a miserable old fart. But it's only for a few weeks − then they can let their hair down."

Gary Barlow also gave the *Mirror* an interview, in his case about how he'd almost walked away from it all the previous year:

> Yeah. It was hard, yeah, yeah. If I'm really honest, I'm not really a fan of hard work. There's a lot of pressure, it really is massive. Last year, I'd sit down feeling so nervous. I was on tour while we were doing the auditions last year and it was hard work. I always felt miserable when I arrived because I was knackered. This year, I've enjoyed the bad ones more than the good ones. I'm almost disappointed when they come out and they're good. I hope to be a bit lighter this year.

(That comment about hard work, incidentally, was a little disingenuous − Gary is one of the most driven stars of his generation.)

Out in the wider world, One Direction's new single, 'Live While We're Young', saw release. While it was not directly related to this year's *X Factor*, the ensuing publicity certainly didn't do it any harm. The band had been watching it, too:

Louis Tomlinson thought Jahmene Douglas would be the one to follow, while Liam Payne rated Ella Henderson. Liam also thought Gary was the best judge – and they all wanted to be judges one day, too.

The acts were beginning to speak out as well. Rylan Clark, a former model from Essex, can't have endeared himself to Nicole when he said that he wished Louis had been his mentor: "If someone had asked me to list the judges in order, I'd have put Louis first," he told *The Sun*. "He knows there's money to be made from people like me. I'm not comparing myself to Jedward – but they didn't have a great first audition and now the kids are worth millions. That's why I wanted Louis." He may well have been right – Louis Walsh was an experienced show-business professional, after all, and it was he who was mentoring the act who would become the series' great success story: Union J.

The Sun capitalised on the growing excitement, featuring brief interviews with a contestant from each of the four categories. From Nicole's camp, they chose 24-year-old guitar player James Arthur: "The whole experience has been like a fairytale. When Nicole sped in on her boat, it was amazing. She's very intelligent and a worldwide superstar. And I think she really believes in me." James himself had experienced a pretty difficult life to date, having spent years in care as a child and only recently talking to his parents again after 22 years: "It was their suggestion I audition," he said. "Maybe they both felt they could have done more for me. I don't feel it's their fault but they probably had a bit of regret and wanted to set me free from that. I hit rock bottom a year ago. I was very depressed and had very little self-belief . . . [now] I want to break the mould of a typical pop star. I feel on top of the world, invincible."

Team Louis featured Stephanie McMichael, 23, a past *Big Brother* contestant, and Sophie Houghton, 21, from Liverpool. "We feel like we're sisters in another life because we know what the other is thinking," said Stephanie. "Past boyfriends have got annoyed when we wanted to do everything together. Geri said we reminded her of Bananarama, so we did 'Venus' next. We didn't know who they were though! We had to look them up."

Chez Gary, Melanie Masson, 44 and a mother of two, stepped out from the crowd. She was another of the contestants who, due to some professional experience, would not have been allowed in previous years. "I've been waking up in a sweat thinking: 'Was it good enough? Did I say anything stupid?'" she said. "You re-live every second. I did a session for a dance record 'featuring Melanie M'. I did two tracks on a Stereophonics album and I was a backing singer for Pink for a few dates. But I could never get that break. It was rejection, rejection. I'd be devastated not to make it to the live shows. But I've loved every second of it so far and so have my kids."

And finally, from Tulisa's camp, there was Jade Collins, 17. "I love Tinie Tempah's music and Tulisa's so cool and down to earth," she said. "But when you're singing, she has her shades on and she's so professional! She doesn't give much away, so that's scary. It really was overwhelming. And yes, I did cry afterwards. I'm mature for my age, so I don't feel like I'm the baby. If I don't get through, I'll be OK . . . but it'll be a long flight home. Someone like me, from Belfast, doesn't get a chance to go to places like this [St Lucia]. I'm at college and work in a café, but I don't want to make sandwiches all my life."

There was serious business to be done in deciding who got through to the next round: Nicole chose 23-year-old Rylan

Clark, a gay ex-model from Essex, Jahmene Douglas, 22, a supermarket worker from Essex, and 23-year-old James Arthur from Middlesbrough, whose difficult times included a period when he was forced to sleep rough.

Tulisa went for schoolgirl Ella Henderson, just 16 and from Lincolnshire (she had only just finished her GCSEs when she first walked out onstage), Lucy Spraggan, 20, from Derbyshire, who sang her own song, and bike mechanic and mother-of-one Jade Ellis from southeast London.

Gary nominated Melanie Masson from Glasgow, who ran a music class for the under-fives, chimney sweep Kye Sones, 30, from London, who used to front electro-pop band Diagram Of The Heart, and 32-year-old Carolynne Poole, a country singer from Huddersfield, who'd split from a relationship with former Manchester United youth player David Poole the previous year. Finally, Louis gave the green light to GMD3, consisting of Greg West, Dan Ferrari-Lane and Mickey Parsons, who met at stage school in London, Union J and MK1, who consisted of dub-step duo Charlotte Rundle and Simeon Dixon.

Given the surprising way in which the boys in Union J were put together, it was their first indication that greater things might just lie ahead. But still their potential was not yet entirely clear. Expectations surrounding the contestants ebbed and flowed, but at that stage of the game the person attracting a good deal of attention was Ella Henderson. "Hearing those comments is crazy – I feel like they aren't talking about me," she told *The Sun*. "It's a very surreal feeling but exciting, too. I've got a constant grin on my face. I will be nervous before the live show but I don't feel pressured. I'm just excited to think I'm still so young and I'm going to be able to keep pushing myself. I've had words with Tulisa about keeping my feet on the ground and I know I can go to her at any point if I feel it's all getting too much."

Everyone else was revelling in it. In the run-up to the big event, Kye Sones was spotted having his teeth whitened; James Arthur was spotted out on a date with Chanelle McCleary, who had appeared on the dating show *Take Me Out*. A whole group – Jade, Lucy, Kye, Carolynne, GMD3 and the boys from Union J – were seen at London's Whisky Mist club, partying away. All of the boys were getting a lot of attention, their first experience of what it was like to be a bona fide celebrity.

To mix it up a little, heightening the suspense and keeping things exciting, at the end of the Judges' Houses segment each judge was told to bring back one act as a wild card, after which the public would vote for a 13th finalist. Nicole chose Adam Burridge, Tulisa went for Amy Mottram, Gary picked Christopher Maloney, who had previously worked as a singer on a cruise ship, and Louis opted for Times Red. It was Gary's choice who eventually got through.

With all the contestants now back in the UK, there was the usual hope of romance among the younger performers; unusually, however, this year there was nothing going on. The contest was dominated by boys; of the girls, Amy and Ella were both only 16 while Jade and Lucy were both lesbians. There was some behind-the-scenes complaining about this from the boys, but in truth, attention from outside the competition was beginning to make up for it. The boys – all of them, not just Union J – were now being recognised in the street. They were appearing regularly on prime-time television, after all, and becoming 'names'. Everyone knew that there were big careers to be had: it was just a matter of who would get to the top. But it was Union J who were increasingly standing out. Charming and talented, it was now becoming clear that they were in with a real chance.

Reports started to suggest that Ella wasn't 'too young' after all, linking her with George Shelley, although both insisted it was nothing more than friendship. Of course, both were still in the competition and boy-band members have been traditionally discouraged from having girlfriends, on the grounds that the fans wouldn't want to think they were unavailable. But that certainly hadn't hurt One Direction's Harry Styles, and there was a counter-argument to the effect that it drummed up good publicity. Whatever the truth at that point, George went on to express his admiration of Demi Lovato – a judge on the US *X Factor*. Harry Styles' image as a womaniser had merely served to highlight his appeal, and the same was looking true of George.

Elsewhere, however, not everything was rosy. One rather less appealing aspect of belonging to a boy band – or being any form of entertainer these days – is the barrage of abuse that comes through Twitter. The most famous example of this concerns just about every woman who was linked to Harry Styles, but it was a fact of life for everyone else involved in the competition too. Both Nicole and Tulisa were regularly given a roasting on Twitter, and now Rylan Clark seemed to be getting his fair share too. Nicole was horrified: "It really frightened and scared me when I got death threats so it upset me to hear Rylan had to go through that pain," she told *The Sun*. "To read some of the comments he has had hurt me too. People need to give Rylan a chance. Everyone that gets to know him has a great fondness and affinity with him."

So were the threats homophobic? Rylan was openly gay, so it was a possibility. And if any member of Union J turned out to be gay, could the same thing happen to him too?

As the live shows neared, everyone involved went all out to

drum up even more publicity for the show. There had always been rumours of rivalry between Gary Barlow and Simon Cowell and, whatever the truth of it, both men knew the value of the publicity. There was speculation that Cowell had deliberately given Barlow the over-28 category, in order for him to appear an old fuddy-duddy himself. There were rumours that Simon was jealous of Gary's hair, a jealousy sparked by a stylist who showed him a poll that listed the most asked-for celebrity hairdos. There were also dark murmurings about what Gary might reveal in his biography. In short, there was almost no area of life in which the two men were said to be at peace with one another.

Meanwhile, Louis, not having anyone specific to feud with at the time, unleashed a bitchathon against Bruce Forsyth who, as a presenter of *Strictly Come Dancing*, worked on a rival Saturday-night show. "It's a good support act for us with a very old singer out front," he told *The Sun*. "He's not exactly young, is he? I won't be on the telly when I'm 84." Then it was on to Andrew Lloyd Webber and last summer's show, *Superstar*. "That was a really bad copy of *X Factor*. Nobody watched it." You couldn't fault him. Louis would have been capable of picking a fight with himself in an empty room if he thought it would drum up publicity for the show.

But then everyone involved was the same – they all knew how much nationwide interest there was and how important it was to keep it up. Days before the live shows began, creative director Brian Friedman gave an interview to *The Sun*; while there wouldn't usually be much interest in what a creative director had to say about anything, this was different – this was *The X Factor* and this was the man charged with knocking One Direction into shape:

Teenage boys are the hardest. I always used to say to the
1D boys: 'One Direction? It's every direction except
where I need you to be!' But being in a room with them
and trying to maintain some level of cooperation kept me
young. We'd rehearse in a gym, but when I needed them
to pay attention they'd throw big yoga balls at each others'
heads. That was their favourite pastime in rehearsals. Harry
was definitely the best dancer; he was always good at the
choreography. Niall was good at remembering which
direction to move in. We all saw at Boot Camp that Zayn
was about to walk away from the competition because of
his dancing, but he's better than he thought.

So was Friedman currently having the same issues with
Union J? He didn't say, but the band was becoming increasingly
polished as the series wore on.

And so it went on: the live-show contestants were also giving
interviews, getting used to this strange new world in which they
found themselves and hoping they were about to hit the big time
at last. Behind the scenes, Union J were rehearsing, giving it
their all and preparing to make the most of an opportunity of a
lifetime. A lot was riding on the next few weeks.

As for the public, there was a palpable sense of expectation.
The live shows were the most exciting part of the competition,
not just because of the suspense that was built up over who
would be the ultimate winner, but also because it was the time
when anything could happen and frequently did. It was when
the judges tended to start rounding on one another, when egos
were punctured and tempers frayed. It was going to require
inner reserves of strength and courage from everyone involved –
but the live shows of the ninth series of *The X Factor* were finally
about to air.

5

The Final Showdown

And so the scene was set.

The live shows were to start on October 6, 2012: each week the contestants were to perform on a Saturday and, in another first for the programme, the voting lines would open before the performances began. This provoked controversy, with some fans labelling the producers as money-hungry (the voting lines charged premium rates), alongside genuine concerns that it might affect the outcome of the votes.

In the previous series, no one could vote for anyone until all the acts had performed; now viewers could do so from the word go, putting the acts that appeared first at a clear advantage and leaving those further down the bill in danger of languishing unloved and ignored. Even so, the producers pressed ahead with the changes and the battle to win the contest began. Ella Henderson was the bookies' favourite to win, with Jahmene Douglas coming in second, but who really knew what would happen? There had been plenty of upsets in the past.

As before, the results were to be announced on Sunday, with the two lowest-rated contestants to be announced. Each would then perform another song of their choice, before the judges decided which to send home. If the judges' votes were tied, then the vote would go to deadlock and the contestant with the fewest votes would be eliminated. Contestants were also allowed to perform their own material, something that had gone down well with the audience in earlier sections of the series.

Each live show was to have a different theme, while the results show would feature a group performance by all contestants who had got through to this point, as well as at least two major star guests – the same calibre of acts who also occasionally performed on the main performance show. Some very big names had been lined up and there was no problem in finding guests; this was prime-time television and it guaranteed massive exposure for everyone.

Britain was still on a high after the success of the Olympic Games, so it made sense to capitalise on the goodwill and kick off with a Heroes' Night theme. Team GB turned out in force: Cowell persuaded no fewer than 11 Olympians to appear, including gymnast Louis Smith, cyclists Victoria Pendleton, Laura Trott, Dani King, Lizzie Armitstead and Joanna Rowsell, boxers Nicola Adams and Luke Campbell, taekwondo ace Jade Jones, rowers Tom James, Pete Reed and Alex Gregory, and dressage champ Charlotte Dujardin. On top of that, 15 Games Makers were also in attendance and the music was to reflect the overall theme. One Direction made an appearance and were interviewed by Dermot O'Leary, although they didn't perform, while the musical guests were Leona Lewis, who sang 'Trouble', and Ne-Yo, who performed 'Let Me Love You (Until You Learn To Love Yourself)'.

Before the performance began, Christopher Maloney was announced as the wild-card vote – and then they were off. In the group category, District3 sang 'The Best', MK1 performed 'Champion'/'Everyone's A Winner' and Union J gave their version of Queen's 'Don't Stop Me Now'. The showdown was between Rylan Clark, who sang 'One Night Only', and Carolynne Poole, who performed 'There You'll Be'. It was the latter who had to leave the show.

It was the showdown which provoked the first of the controversies to dog the finals, with some increasingly fractious and bad tempered behaviour on display. Louis prevaricated for some time before finally making up his mind. First he said he wanted to "keep Carolynne"; Dermot asked him if that meant Rylan was to leave; "I want to keep them both," said Louis. O'Leary asked him to clarify and Walsh decided to take the vote to deadlock. Carolynne was thus eliminated, as she'd received the fewest public votes. Gary, her mentor, promptly accused, "This is a joke," and stormed off.

The public wasn't happy either, especially when it emerged that Richard Holloway had a word with Louis during Carolynne's final performance, with the suggestion that it might have influenced Louis in some way. Gary announced on *The Xtra Factor* that it was "disgusting" how a talented singer had been eliminated in favour of a "joke act" – presumably a reference to Rylan's flamboyance; meanwhile, 2,500 complaints were made to Ofcom and ITV. Holloway was forced to issue a clarification, the second time he had done so on the show:

> We regularly chat to the judges during the show, they don't wear earpieces like Dermot so we have to speak to them on anything from timings to running order changes. On Sunday I was telling Louis the order the judges would vote in. We don't tell judges how to vote.

In the following week the theme was love and heartbreak, with musical guests Rebecca Ferguson singing 'Backtrack' and Taylor

Swift performing 'We Are Never Going To Get Back Together'. In the group category, District3 sang 'I Swear', MK1 did 'I Want You Back' and Union J put in an extremely impressive performance of 'Bleeding Love'/'Broken Strings'. The act was really beginning to come together. They were "a total transformation from last week", an impressed Gary told them. Meanwhile, in the group category, District3 did so badly that they ended up in the bottom two – although in the end it was Melanie Masson who left. "I'm gutted," said Gary. "She's one of the best singers in the competition. I thought she was the safest of my acts this weekend."

Once again, controversy broke out. Tulisa set it off this time. Praising Melanie's rendition of 'Never Tear Us Apart', she added, "You are in full MILF mode!" She didn't spell out what the acronym meant and it was said at 10.30 p.m., well after the watershed, but cautious *X Factor* bosses weren't taking any chances.

"I want to apologise for the language Tulisa used," Dermot O'Leary duly announced. "Naughty, naughty, but that's why we love her." This in itself prompted outrage, however, when it was pointed out that Tulisa had not used a swear word and anyway, it was late at night – Twitter was soon ablaze with the issue. Viewers were also unhappy that parts of Rylan's performance were cut from repeat broadcasts, including the recap of his phone vote number, although it was due to complicated copyright reasons according to the producers.

Week three had as its theme club classics, with the 11 remaining contestants performing dance anthems. The guests were Labrinth, featuring Emeli Sandé singing 'Beneath Your Beautiful', and JLS, who performed 'Hottest Girl In The World'; the group performance was of Chaka Khan's 'Ain't Nobody'. In the group category, MK1 sang 'Gypsy Woman (She's Homeless)'/ 'Pass Out', District3 went for 'Beggin''/'Turn Up The Music', and Union J performed David Guetta and Kelly Rowland's 'When Love Takes Over'. MK1 and Kye were in the final showdown – which MK1 lost after the result was deadlocked, having the lowest share of votes.

There were some emotional scenes when MK1 went. Now that there were less than a dozen acts left it was getting a lot more personal, and there were now only two left in the group category. Union J were still facing plenty of competition but the focus on them was sharper than ever. The week wore on with intensive rehearsals. They had the capacity to make a huge impact, as Nicole Scherzinger clearly believed: "Don't underestimate them," she said in an interview with *The Sun*. By now, bookies were giving odds of 7-1 that Union J would win.

Simon Cowell was also beginning to take an interest in their performance. Cowell was riding extremely high on the success of another of his signings, One Direction, and it was said that he was becoming a little alarmed that these new upstarts might pose a threat to his protégés. Union J was startled, but highly amused.

"I loved that Simon was threatened by us," Jaymi told the *Daily Star Sunday*. "I rang Louis straight away and asked what he said. Louis said Simon was threatened because he has a boy band this year who could topple his. Simon has got the groups on US *X Factor* so he's trying to get his own new One Direction from America. But Louis has got his game face on this year, so I think there is an extra bit of competition between Simon and Louis. Louis has told us he's determined to win. It's nice that we are still on Simon's radar even though he isn't on the show this year."

This seems a little disingenuous – although it's also possible that Jaymi didn't realise Cowell was in a win/win situation. If

One Direction downed the competition, then he would prosper; if Union J looked as if they might snatch the 1D crown – well, Simon was going to sign them too. They might be Louis' pet project on the show, but when the time came to sign management deals Simon would be waiting in the wings, contracts at the ready. There was no way he was going to miss out on the success of stars created by his own TV show.

In fact, Ella was still the favourite to win and the rumours continued to circulate about her and George. "Yes, I admit we do really like each other," she said in an interview with the *Daily Star Sunday*. "It's hard because our schedules are so busy that you don't have time for a romance . . . but you never know after the show. Everyone keeps telling me how cute we are together and we do have so much in common. We really get along and he's my best friend." That seemed to be the truth of it – but it suited everyone involved to keep the possibility of a romance alive. It was all for the good of the show.

Week four saw the biggest guest star to date. Robbie Williams had been a guest judge on the programme the previous year, alongside his friend and former bandmate Gary, and was in a good position to offer advice to nascent boy bands.

Union J seemed in need of a little advice themselves, for that week they ended up in the final showdown – although in the event it was Jade Ellis who had to say goodbye. The judges felt that the boys had to dare to be different though.

"I think the vocals were really good tonight, you did a really good job," said Tulisa. "But my issue is that you played it a little bit safe. I thought you could have done something a bit more exciting."

"For me, it was safe," said Gary. "Surprise us, guys. Come back with something different. Change it up."

Hug a hoodie: JJ Hamblett.
(CARON WESTBROOK AND JULIAN WHITE)

Strike a pose: Josh Cuthbert.
(CARON WESTBROOK AND JULIAN WHITE)

Nice tattoo see you: Jaymi Hensley.
(CARON WESTBROOK AND JULIAN WHITE)

The Rewind line-up.
(CARON WESTBROOK AND JULIAN WHITE)

The boys at Whiskey Mist, September 2012.
(PHOTOFAB/REX FEATURES)

Who you talkin' to? The boys on *Daybreak* in October 2012.
(KEN MCKAY/REX FEATURES)

The name's... Union J. At the 2012 *Skyfall* premiere in London.
(REX FEATURES)

But Nicole stood up for them. "Well boys, I thought that was absolute perfection," she acclaimed. "I thought it was brilliant. It was simple, it was beautiful." They would stay in the game.

Jade was far from thrilled, opining that the judges were only seeking to protect themselves. "I don't think the decision on Sunday was based entirely on the sing-off," she told *The Sun*. "The judges were thinking about their own acts. I believe I sang that song to a really high standard and if that wasn't enough to save me I honestly don't know what I could have done. People have said my performance was better than Union J's, but Tulisa was out there on her own when she chose to put me through. The vote could have been tactical. Maybe the judges thought Union J were less of a threat to their singers in the competition. It is getting to that point in the game where the judges all criticise each other's acts. But whatever the reasoning, I don't think they did it lightly."

It was certainly true that, by this stage, everyone involved was beginning to take a close commercial interest in the acts and a personable young boy band was an attractive proposition. In fact they were growing in popularity by the day.

But both Robbie Williams' presence and the absence of Lucy Spraggan, due to illness (or, according to rumour, behind-the-scenes wrangling over her desire to sing her own music), were overshadowed by yet another bout of bad tempered behaviour from the judges. Christopher Maloney had just been performing; Tulisa turned to Gary and said, "You do the same thing over and over again with him and it's not working."

"Tulisa," Gary replied, "I don't know what's offended me more – what you said or the fag ash breath."

Tulisa was clearly taken aback and sat for a moment looking stunned, before interrupting Dermot a moment later to say,

"Just a note for Gary – lay off the red wine because I can really smell that as well."

Of course, part of the fun of *The X Factor* lies in watching the judges bicker, but it was felt that Gary had gone too far. What he'd just said was not gentlemanly: you just didn't tell a woman on prime-time television that she had bad breath. The two of them appeared on *The Xtra Factor* together and it was apparent that Gary had been eating humble pie. Had he also been drinking red wine?

"A little sip," he confirmed, before continuing. "Can I apologise to Tulisa – I mean it. You have the freedom to be as personal as you like to me for the rest of the series – insult me."

Tulisa added that Gary had once said he loved the smell of cigarettes, as it reminded him of his smoking days. Gary hastily agreed, before she was asked if she was all right with him. "Yeah, we're good, yeah, of course," she replied. The crisis was over; the show could go on.

By this time, interest in Union J was such that the boys required additional security. It had happened twice now that fans had broken into the hotel they were staying in; although they had been removed, there were concerns that they might actually get to the boys. The fans were cunning too. The hotel reported receiving about 50 CVs from young girls looking for bar work and (although they didn't spell it out) the chance to meet the band. The boys themselves were now using secret entrances to avoid being mobbed. Matters took a more ominous turn when George's laptop was stolen from the hotel – with information about the boys increasingly sought after, security had to be increased even more.

They weren't complaining, though. This was a foretaste of the stardom that might become theirs. But it also caused problems.

George and Ella were spotted walking hand in hand and were mobbed when they tried to get back inside – but they were emphatically not a couple, they claimed.

"It's purely platonic," insisted George. "She's like my little sister."

Still, it drummed up great publicity for the show. Union J were mobbed when they went shopping on Oxford Street and similar hysteria greeted their announcement of an appearance at Brent Cross shopping centre. Although they waited until the last minute before making their appearance, thousands of fans turned out to meet them – so many that it had to be called off amid safety fears. Behind the scenes, they also met One Direction, the people to whom they were so often compared. Harry Styles gave George Shelley some very sound advice: "Don't cut your curls."

The theme for week five was, appropriately enough, number ones; the guest stars were Rita Ora and No Doubt. Union J was safe that week, with a rendition of Taylor Swift's 'Love Story'; the final showdown was between Rylan Clark and Kye Sones, who left. The contest was halfway over now, with seven acts left. The tension was rising.

However, controversy continued to rage behind the scenes. Given that he had been a wild card, Christopher Maloney had been doing very well indeed, although he raised an awful lot of hackles when he admitted he had been consistently voting for himself on the show. This was not against the show's rules, but it was felt to be not quite the done thing. Kye, who had only just left, sounded very bitter, claiming Chris "must have an expensive phone bill" and that his behaviour was "very tactical".

Chris was totally unrepentant. "I have voted for myself a few times," he told the *Daily Mirror*. "So has everyone else – I doubt my calls have made much of a difference. If I had more credit on my phone I'd vote more."

No one from the show would comment publicly, but eyebrows were very much raised. Off the record, one insider told the paper that Chris had been seen dialling and redialling his own number over and over again. Unnamed sources called him "desperate" and said the show's bosses were furious. "You can't outlaw this sort of behaviour, but it leaves a very sour taste," said one. "It's against the spirit of the show." Given that it wasn't against the rules, however, nothing could be done and Christopher went on to fight another day.

Week six featured the 'Best Of British'. There was considerable excitement when it emerged that One Direction were to guest on the Saturday show, with Ed Sheeran and Little Mix following on Sunday night. (In fact One Direction's appearance had been taped a couple of weeks earlier, something that would upset a few viewers.)

Union J sang Coldplay's 'Fix You'. They then landed in the final showdown against District3. Louis, who was a mentor to both of them, refused to vote, and so it was left to Gary and Tulisa to send District3 home.

Week seven (which was also the week that Jaymi came out as gay) had as its theme 'Guilty Pleasures', featuring guests Olly Murs and Alicia Keys. Union J performed well with Carly Rae Jepsen's 'Call Me Maybe', while James Arthur and Ella Henderson took part in the final showdown – to everyone's shock, it was former favourite Ella who left. The vote had been deadlocked and she received the lowest number of votes from the public.

No one was more taken aback by this outcome than the members of Union J. "That was the biggest shock ever in *X Factor* history," said George.

"It was bittersweet for us because we were chuffed to get through but they are our two best friends in the show," added Josh. "We've got so close, so we were devastated – it was like watching your big brother and your little sister in the sing-off. We were gutted for Ella – we were in tears backstage, we absolutely adore her."

There was also further controversy caused by the judges' behaviour, in this case Nicole, who introduced her protégé by saying: "This is James effing Arthur!" This was pre-watershed and did not go down well. As was becoming the custom in this series, she apologised on *The Xtra Factor*. "I'm so sorry," she said. "You spend every day with these people, you spend so much time with them. Ella was the last female in the competition. I was passionate about her as well as James Arthur, who is one of the greatest human talents ever. I'm so sorry for my 'effing'." She was forgiven.

And so on to week eight. The themes were Abba and Motown; the guests were Bruno Mars and Rihanna. Union J initially sang 'The Winner Takes It All', followed by The Jackson 5's 'I'll Be There', but there was a brush with danger when they ended up in the final showdown with Rylan Clark. Nicole, Rylan's mentor, was the only one to vote for Union J to leave, and so they would fight another day. Tulisa spelt the reasoning out: they had more potential to sell records, she said. They most certainly did and now, so very close to the final, the stakes could not have been higher.

The band themselves were well aware of just how far they'd come. "Week one we sat at the soundcheck and said, 'We are the weakest act here' – because we were!" Jaymi told *The Sun*. "So now, to have got to the quarter-finals and be up against James Arthur and Jahmene Douglas and not be the weakest act is amazing. We've really progressed."

"We really thought we were only here to make up the numbers," JJ said. "But now we feel we're right in the middle of things." They were right.

Week nine was the semi-final, with just four acts left: Union J, Christopher Maloney, Jahmene Douglas and James Arthur. The theme was 'songs for someone special', followed by qualifiers for the final with no particular theme at all. Each act sang two songs: Union J went with 'Beneath Your Beautiful' and Lonestar's 'I'm Already There' (as covered by Westlife); Christopher sang 'You Raise Me Up' and 'Haven't Met You Yet'; Jahmene performed 'I Look To You' and 'At Last'; James Arthur gave his renditions of 'One' and 'The Power Of Love'. The guests were Pink, who sang 'Try', and none other than Tulisa, who stepped out from behind the judges' desk to perform 'Sight Of You'. Every show had seen a group performance and this one was no different: they banded together to sing 'Merry Christmas Baby', joined by another very famous guest – Rod Stewart. This week there were to be no judges' decisions – it was simply a case of the act with the fewest public votes leaving.

And so it was that, having got so very close to the prize, Union J left the show.

The boys took it very well. They sang their rendition of 'Love Story' and were joined by their mentor, Louis, onstage to say their goodbyes. They could hardly have been more dignified. "I'm so happy with how well we've done," said Josh. "We've got so much to thank *X Factor* for."

JJ was magnanimous: "We wanna wish the guys the best of luck," he said of the remaining contestants.

"I can't describe how amazing it's been," said Jaymi.

Indeed, it was only Louis who expressed regret. "I'm a little disappointed, but we were ready for it," he said. "They're going to be the next big boy band."

No one could dispute that. While winning would have been nice, in truth Union J no longer had any need to get to the top slot. They'd had months of exposure on prime-time television, consistently shown what they were capable of and already built up quite a following. The show was far from over.

After they'd had time to digest it, it didn't take the boys long to understand that not winning might actually work in their favour. "Nine times out of 10 it is actually better not to win," Jaymi told *The Sun*, citing such other 'losers' as One Direction, Cher Lloyd, JLS and Olly Murs. "It is exciting times for Union J. We get the option to really work on our artistry. We get the time but not the pressure of being the winners to really sit down and work out what style of music we want to do and make us a brand. We have got a lot of positives out of this and they outweigh the negatives."

"We hope this is just the start of Union J's career and hopefully we can go on and do what One Direction and JLS have done," said Josh.

And so, along with the rest of the country, Union J settled back to see who would actually win the ninth series of *The X Factor*. The final was held in Manchester, the first time it had taken place outside London. For the first night, the guests were Kelly Clarkson, Rita Ora and Kylie Minogue. There was to be no theme, other than duets with the mentors. Jahmene sang 'Move On Up', followed by 'The Greatest Love Of All' with Nicole; Christopher Maloney sang 'Flashdance . . . What A Feeling' and 'Rule The World' with Gary; James sang 'Feeling Good' and 'Make You Feel My Love' with Nicole. Christopher Maloney was eliminated and did not take it well.

For the second show, on Sunday, all the finalists got together for a group performance of 'I Wish It Could Be Christmas Everyday', 'Last Christmas' and 'Santa Claus Is Coming To Town'. Three acts were missing: MK1, Lucy and Christopher.

That last absence was the subject of a lot of comment. It was said that Christopher had been excluded for turning up late at rehearsals and smelling of alcohol. He also got into a very hostile Twitter exchange with Carolynne Poole, heaping abuse on her; Carolynne in turn tweeted that *The X Factor* "can also create monsters".

A spokesman for the show declared: "Chris decided he no longer wanted to be part of *The X Factor* final and has gone back to Liverpool."

Chris himself took to Twitter again to defend himself against allegations of unprofessional behaviour: "@TheXFactor @xfactorpress @GBarlowOfficial can't believe all the bull yet again! this is a witch hunt for defo. the show is over xx

"yes I am being bullied! big time. there u go xx witch hunt xx"

He also denied that he'd stormed out: "thank u all so much for ur love help and support. thinking everyone wants a final dig. disgusting xx love u na nite xx

"sorry I had a sore throat an doctor signed me off. good luck x"

And with that he was gone.

At the final, Jahmene sang 'Angels' and 'Let It Be'; James sang 'Let's Get It On' and 'Impossible', before being declared the winner. He was to release 'Impossible' as his debut single; had they won, Union J would have released Demi Lovato's 'Skyscraper'.

But in every way that was crucial to their future career, Union

J actually had won. They had given a sensational performance the whole way through and clearly had a brilliant future ahead.

So who were these boys who had sprung into the limelight? Just who *are* Union J?

6

The Musical Prodigy

Sometimes talent runs in the family. In the UK, the Redgraves are a successful acting dynasty, the late author Sir Kingsley Amis was the father of equally famous novelist Martin and the three Brontë sisters all produced masterpieces. In the US, the Kennedys dominated politics for so long that they were the nearest the States had come to a royal family.

It would be overegging the pudding to say that George Shelley comes from quite such an illustrious background, but it's equally true that talent runs in his family. His grandfather, Dave, was a police officer by training but would play the guitar and accordion in his spare time; he still plays the latter at old people's homes.

His uncle, Jon Harris, is a singer-songwriter and musician, while two other uncles, Tim and Tom, are drummers.

His mother, Toni Harris, is a nurse and aerobics teacher, but she too plays the guitar, writes music and has performed at festivals and small venues. It would have been surprising if George had not inherited the musical gene – but in fact his talents were to become clear from a very early age.

George Shelley was born on July 27, 1993, at Southmead Hospital in Clevedon, to Toni and Dominic. Clevedon is a small town in north Somerset, among a small group of hills running alongside the River Severn estuary; it's now a popular seaside town with a seafront boasting ornamental gardens, a Victorian bandstand and a light railway. Clevedon Pier was one of the first to be built in the Victorian era, and the town also saw the first large-scale production of penicillin.

George is the third of four children, named after an elderly gentleman his mother used to nurse. The eldest son, Tom, now lives in Australia; he has worked as a builder but is also a talented musician. (As of spring 2013, he is on the verge of releasing a single.) The second brother, William, is four years older than George and is now a Royal Marine, based in Cardiff, who has served in Afghanistan. He contracted meningitis when his little brother was going through the *X Factor* audition process, but made a full recovery. George's sister, Harriet, is three years younger than him and currently studying for her A-levels.

George was a precocious child, as well he might be with so many fellow musicians in the family. He played drums from an early age and his mother used to fill up bottles with rice, so that he could play them as maracas. "We have a musical family and his granddad Dave was a real rock'n'roller," his mother told the *Bristol Post*. "George, even as a young boy, always wanted to join in and used to pretend he was playing on the drums, using a saucepan and a wooden spoon. We also used to make instruments by filling up washing up bottles with rice. He has always loved singing, dancing and playing instruments and enjoyed drama and being in plays. He has always been the sort of person who could pick up an instrument and play it – a talent he got from his granddad."

The ability to pick up tunes easily was to stand him in very good stead. It was George who, much more than the rest of

Union J, would have to make a huge shift in direction to turn from a solo singer into a band member. Moreover, he would have to fit in with a group of people who had been working together for some time, even if they had not been rehearsing as much as early manager Kasey Monroe thought they should.

Surrounded by so many family members who encouraged and nurtured his musicality, George had begun to make great leaps while he was still quite young. All he really needed was someone to guide him along the right path, which he was to find when not yet out of his teens.

He would be the youngest member of Union J. As the baby of the group – much as he was the second youngest member of his family – he would learn to fit in with the rest. His innate musicality made him an invaluable asset for the band, while a cheerful spirit and readiness to take new experiences onboard would also stand him in good stead.

George was so precociously talented that he first gained a taste for the limelight as a tiny child. "He has played with me at the Burnham Acoustic Club and he did his first performance there aged five or six," his grandfather, Dave, told the *Weston Mercury*. "The first couple of times he performed on his own, then we got together to play and we were also joined by his older brother from Australia, who is a drummer. It went down very well, but every time George played solo he got the biggest reception. He has a natural gift. When he was growing up he was in the background and had a lot to compete with, as he came from such a large crowd, and seeing him performing now makes us feel very proud."

Fighting to stand out in a large crowd: it was almost as if Dave was describing a kind of vocational training for *The X Factor*. It also accounts for George's ease and natural ability onstage. He had been accustomed to audiences right from the time he was a toddler, and he had started performing for a wider public around the time most children are starting school. George's precocity meant that he was bound to have a performing career of some kind.

But he did not, however, have any professional training. "George sang as soon as he could talk and is able to harmonise perfectly," Toni told Weston College in an interview posted on its website, after *The X Factor* began and it emerged that George had been a pupil. "He's never had a guitar lesson in his life but he's got a natural ability and took part in Priddy Folk Festival at just 14."

He also attended quite a few schools: back when he was a toddler, he was at the Happy Hours Day Nursery in Nailsea, followed by Backwell Infant School, Golden Valley Primary School and Yeo Moor School in Clevedon. As a teenager he went on to study at the King Alfred School in Burnham-on-Sea, followed by Kings of Wessex at Cheddar.

His home life was a peripatetic existence that made it hard for George to form any long-lasting friendships. "I went to a lot of schools because we moved house quite a lot," he'd confirm. "I never had the chance to make any solid friends but I always had my guitar so I was OK." His love of music was to fill the gap. Toni and Dominic split up when George was just three, but Dominic continued to play a big role in his son's life and took him to his first ever concert, a Bon Jovi bash.

Simon Aylward, now assistant head teacher at King Alfred School, was George's form master, and remembers a quiet little boy who kept his musical talents well and truly hidden from his peers.

"He kept to a small group of friends," he says. "They were

mostly boys. He was very quiet, not sporty, and spent his time with like-minded friends. They were not of interest to the girls. There were some vivacious students but they never showed interest in George. He had big glasses and long hair, back then."

Mr Aylward is too polite to spell it out, but George was also very plump – something he has himself admitted. He showed no musical talent at school and never performed in assemblies, so the powers that be didn't know of the talent waiting to burst out. Neither did he appear to have many hobbies, and he certainly couldn't be said to stand out from the crowd.

But it is often the case that the shy and the modest are the ones who ultimately make an impact, as many of the really popular types at school do not live up to their early promise. In George's case, he would come into his own when he had lost the weight and ditched the glasses, in his late teens.

"He was reasonably academic, in the middle somewhere," Simon Aylward continues. "He hadn't really thought about what he would be doing and there was no clear indication where he would go in life. It's difficult to equate him with what he looks like now and what he looked like then and I couldn't have imagined him wanting to be in front of a crowd. He was not an extrovert. There is a big difference in his manner now – he has clearly got confidence over the years. We were all very surprised when we realised it was him on *X Factor*, but good luck to him now."

George left in 2007, just before GCSEs, to start at yet another school in the locality. It might not have come out back then – he was doubtless too shy to show off in front of his fellow school-mates – but his musical talent was still being strongly cultivated at home.

"My wife and I bought George his first guitar for his 14th

birthday," Dave told the *Weston Mercury*. "We have always had musical instruments about the place. We have always had a piano in the living room and there was also a guitar lying about the house. He's a bright lad and he always used to tinkle about on the instruments. I think this helped George, he's obviously been influenced by one thing and another and it gave him confidence as well. It put him on the right path."

It certainly did. George could now go off and practise on his own for hours, honing the techniques that would one day stand him in such good stead. It gave him much more focus and an ability to proceed on his own, even without the formal training that two of his later band members would have. In the meantime, he also took part in plays at school, giving him more valuable experience to put to good use when he was older.

But George's childhood was not always a happy one. He was bullied at school, he'd recall later in life (although he didn't specify which school). He had gained a lot of weight, which made him a target for bullies, and was not as interested in sport as the rest of them, which didn't help either. His problems back then affect his self-image to this day, but he was forced to develop a steely inner resilience.

Just as Jaymi would later provide a role model for gay teenagers finding it difficult to confront their sexuality, so George could provide hope for bullied children that they would one day come out ahead. If he got through it and went on to become extremely successful, so could they.

"I was 12 stone and really short," he told the *Daily Star*. "All the other boys loved football and I just wanted to play my guitar. I was always the last one picked because no one wanted the fatty who couldn't run. The worst thing that happened was we were playing football and one of the kids purposefully kicked the ball as hard as they could right at me. I put my hands up to protect my face and ended up breaking my wrist."

Nor was he particularly successful with girls back then, something that would be greeted with frank incredulity when the boys stepped into the spotlight. But it could well have been the resultant teenage angst that pushed him on.

It is a well known fact that many of the most successful people in life had difficult early lives – Tom Cruise and Kate Winslet were both bullied in their teens – and it is the urge to show the bullies they were wrong that drives their ultimate success. So it was with George. There was also something of the male ugly duckling syndrome: he might have been short and plump back then, but as he slimmed down and grew into his looks, with hair to rival that of the great Harry Styles, he was always going to have the last laugh.

However, the bullying did leave him with a bad body image. Incredible as it may seem for someone who became a heart-throb, George remained unable to accept that he was attractive and was very reticent about his appearance.

"I was obese, I'm massively insecure," he told *Heat*. "I won't even take my top off in the pool. It's programmed into my head that I'm fat because I got bullied at school and I can't get it out. If I got changed for PE and took my top off, people would laugh. If we went sunbathing, we'd probably wear wetsuits."

In yet another twist of fate, when the boys first appeared on *The X Factor*, it was George who was dubbed the 'womaniser' of the group by the press, which sits at odds with that negative self-image.

However, all that was still to come. When George was still at his studies, more problems arose within his family. In 2011, his mother, Toni, suffered a stroke. Initially dismissed as just a migraine, when Toni was sent home from hospital her brain continued to bleed, leading to loss of feeling on her left side. It would not be the end of her troubles: in 2012, Toni had surgery on both wrists for carpal tunnel syndrome, leaving her unable to work.

It was a difficult time for all the family, but George persevered with his plans for the future. Although his love of music and performing was as strong as ever, he had no professional training and the idea of making a full-time career of it didn't occur to him. Instead, he completed his schooling and started to prepare for a professional qualification. He hoped to travel abroad (a wish that would be fulfilled beyond his wildest dreams, although not quite in the way he'd anticipated) and to live a fulfilling professional life. His family would all be very supportive of him – but to the extent that they later doubted the wisdom of entering *The X Factor*.

George went to Weston College, a further education establishment based in Weston-super-Mare, with about 7,500 students split between campuses there and at Nailsea. He also had a part-time job as a barista at Costa Coffee in Weston-super-Mare. "For a while my life was all about serving coffee to people, standing behind a till and just dreaming of singing for a job," George later recalled. "All four of us in the band keep saying how unreal everything is."

Back then though, dreams of stardom seemed as far away as the moon. George was a typical student and there was little that hinted at what was to follow. By this time, however, he had come into his looks. The puppy fat had dropped off, leaving George a lean, trim young man. His acne had cleared up, revealing not only a fine complexion but cheekbones too. His teeth were shiny and white, his eyes large and dark, and his hair, his crowning glory, was worthy of Harry Styles, to whom he would be so frequently compared.

He was turning into a boy who could easily be a teen heartthrob – which is crucial because, no matter how talented the singer, it is never going to work if he doesn't have the look. But George did. He was developing the appeal that would make young girls want to date him and older women want to mother him, in exactly the right proportions for the career he was shortly to embark upon.

George would develop the curious combination of being a boy next door-cum-superstar, both ordinary and extraordinary at the same time. No matter how well he did, he would never lose the approachability factor or allow any of it to go to his head. None of the boys seemed to quite believe what had happened to them but it was especially the case with George, who was always engagingly well aware of his luck.

By this stage of his life he had also confirmed all his personal tastes, the details of which fans would one day devour so voraciously: he likes Marmite with the right amount of butter, Jaffa cakes, coffee and watching *Star Trek* with his mother; he prefers brown sugar to white; his favourite food is spaghetti bolognese; his favourite colour is red; he is a fan of horror films; he likes *The Big Bang Theory*, in which his favourite character is Sheldon; his favourite cartoon character is Ash Ketchum from *Pokemon*; he prefers the iPhone to a Blackberry ("Let's face it, who doesn't!" was one fan website's response to that particular nugget of information); he has tattoos of a lion and a monkey (his favourite animal) on his bum; his favourite song is 'Live It Up' by Tulisa – although this was only revealed after he met her on the show.

But at that stage, studying was on his mind. George completed a BTEC extended diploma in graphic design, his chosen career at that point, and was about to start a second year at Bath Spa University. "I had a great time at Weston College and my tutors were fantastic," he later said in a listing on the college website. "I got the chance to go to New York while on the course and that was very memorable."

He was remembered very fondly as well. "I am so proud of George," said his tutor, Rachael Heath, "he has such talent and determination, I wish him so much luck and all the votes he could wish for."

When he was at college, the intention was to return to the United States to work – but then *The X Factor* came up. It was a big decision to make: abandon studies for the hope of fame? Or perhaps take a gap year?

Graphic design promised a good career to choose, while the world of show business was fickle, competitive and very difficult. But of course, making it in show business also offered the kind of rewards unavailable elsewhere. On the other hand, Toni's recent illnesses had brought home how a steady income was highly desirable – although George now had to think about a choice he had never conceived before.

Initially, it didn't even occur to him to audition, but his friend Emily Tollner, who knew how musical he was, told him he should give it a go. To his own great astonishment, he got through. George didn't initially tell his family, not really believing he was in with a chance until he made it through to the final audition for a place on the show. Up until then, the thought of appearing on one of prime-time television's biggest shows had been mere fantasy.

There was no hiding it from the family any more – on a practical level, he was going to be spending a lot of time away from home and, fairly soon, the entire country was going to see him onscreen. George broke the news to Toni who, after the initial shock, said she would accompany him to London, where he was told he had made it to Boot Camp. He wowed the judges with a rendition of Britney Spears' 'Toxic': "You have a great look and a great vocal," said Louis. George had clearly made an impression; from that point onwards, Louis, for one, was keen to keep him on the show.

It was there that George joined Triple J, which promptly turned into Union J. George was the youngest and newest member of the band, but from the word go they all got on. The outcome was nearly very different, however.

The news came through that he was to be given a second shot at it when George was at home with his mother. Having initially failed to make it through to the Judges' Houses round, the dejected wannabe had returned home under the impression that that was that. His dream of a career in show business was not to be.

And then – a miracle happened.

George had not been a party to the backstage manoeuvrings, and had no idea the producers were about to perform the televisual equivalent of pulling a rabbit out of a hat. He was stunned by it all.

"The phone rang and George mouthed to me 'It's *The X Factor* on the phone,'" Toni told the *Bristol Post* in October 2012, before it had become clear just how successful Union J was going to be. "Someone from the show had rung up asking him back. His face was so taut – he was so tense. He turned to me and said he had an hour to call them back and if he agreed he had to be in London the next morning."

He called them back.

7

A Band Meant To Be

What happened next seems almost like fate. Contrary to popular belief, George did not go straight to Triple J, as they then were. Instead, the *X Factor* bosses suggested he try his luck with MK1.

It was MK1 member Charlie Rundle who vetoed that one: "The media made out I was forced into [Union J], but I wasn't," George told *Heat* magazine. "The *X Factor* producers wanted to put me in MK1, but Charlie, the female singer in that band, wouldn't let me. She didn't think I'd fit in. So the producers said I could either go in GMD3 or Triple J."

What would have happened if George had linked up with MK1? We will never know. But the right result was arrived at in the end (although it's hard to believe that MK1 wouldn't kick themselves in the fullness of time).

In any case, events now began to move fast. Quite a few people were thinking alike, for the *X Factor* bosses were not the only people who had spotted George's potential. He had also caught the eye of music-scene insider Blair Dreelan, who immediately realised that George had the potential to go far. Dreelan also had a band on his hands, called Triple J.

"When George got kicked off the show I got in talks to manage him because I just thought he was great and looked like a pop star, I thought he could be developed into a pop star," Blair told sugarscape.com. "Then two weeks later *The X Factor* called me and were like, 'How do you feel about putting a fourth member into the band?' I said, 'It really depends on who it is,' and they went, 'We've got this kid called George and he got kicked off the show,' and I said, 'Well I've got this kid now called George who got kicked out the show.' They were like, '180,000 people entered this show: it can't be the same George.' So I emailed them a picture while I was on the phone to them and they were like, 'Wow, it's amazing, it's almost like fate, exactly the same kid.' Even when I'm telling you this story now I'm getting goosebumps because it was just such a strange thing to happen. And from then it was really, really quick, an overnight thing."

Even if *The X Factor* hadn't put all five of them together, it's entirely possible that they would have linked up at some stage anyway, given that they were all managed by the same person. At the very least, there would have been some ongoing contact between the four.

This was not the only way in which fate seemed to be playing a part. The members of Triple J had also noticed George – so much so that they were already considering the possibility of collaboration before either Blair or the *X Factor* bosses put it to them.

"The other weird thing was – this was really, really strange – when they got back from the first stage of Boot Camp Jaymi was on his iPad and he was like, 'There was this kid that was at the Boot Camp that was amazing, he just looked amazing,'" Blair continued. "And what he'd done was crop four pictures of the boys together with George in the band before George was actually in the band. So it was like a chain of really spooky events. Then we had these four days, the boys were really excited when

I told them because it was obviously the same kid they'd seen in the picture that they met at Boot Camp and built a little bit of a friendship. They didn't know each other but they kind of talked. And then I, obviously knowing Josh really well, knew that his personality and George's personality were very similar; I knew that Josh would get on really well with him and the other boys would as well. So I pulled him in four days before we went to Judges' Houses and had this day, which was a getting to know each other day."

And so history was made.

The X Factor had thought it a good idea to link them all up; Blair had exactly the same idea and, if that were not enough, Jaymi was putting them all together on his iPad before any final decisions had been made. Not only was it clearly fated to be, it also made matters considerably easier for George. The boys were extremely welcoming from the start. They were an established trio and he was an outsider, but to have so many people telling him it was a match made in boy-band heaven smoothed the transit massively. Not only was George now in the band, he knew that everyone wanted him there too.

By this time, everyone was feeling a great deal of strain. When they had all started, there had been nothing to lose; no one had anything to prove; there were also several hundred acts at the outset, and it would be no shame to have failed to get picked from such a huge range of competition. George could easily have gone back to college; the others could have tried their luck elsewhere.

But things were different now. By the time the acts got to the Judges' Houses segment of the show, there was all to play for and a real chance of winning. The boys were determined to make it through.

"It's been really hard work," said Toni Shelley as the finals were about to get under way. "They work very hard and get very tired, but [George is] loving every minute of it. He loves the judges and says they are all really supportive. But the one thing he does want is a home-cooked roast dinner."

It was all so public. This wasn't just any old talent competition. If there was a mess-up now, it was going to happen in the full public gaze and there would be nowhere to hide. All the boys had the support of their local communities, which meant that families and friends were watching the show and would know immediately of any disasters that might befall them. So indeed was the wider community. There was no place to hide when you went on *The X Factor*, as the boys were beginning to discover.

Indeed, it was taking its toll on the whole family almost as much as it was on George. Everything had to be kept top secret, even from the nearest and dearest. The families had not been told who got through from the Judges' Houses, and so Toni waited and fretted back home. The family knew they would be going to collect George from the airport, but would he be delighted or dejected? Was he returning from triumph or despair?

It was only when they finally met him at Gatwick that they heard the good news. "We were all there sitting in Costa Coffee waiting for the contestants to get off the plane," Toni recalled. "We still at that stage didn't know whether they had got through. But then I saw George and he shouted 'yes' and then there was lots of hugging and kissing."

Now a really serious decision had to be made. Should George continue with his studies or decide that his real path in life lay in being a pop star? It had started to become evident that Union J had a real future, whether they won *The X Factor* or not. Until now, the option had existed for George to return to his studies, perhaps even taking a gap year and going back afterwards; but if he continued with Union J, he was making a definite choice: no more graphic design. George knew he wanted to carve out a career in the world of music, but even so, it was taking quite a risk.

But this was a dream opportunity of a kind that many musicians never receive in a whole lifetime. If he didn't take it, George knew that he would face a lifetime of regret. But not everyone was convinced he was doing the right thing.

"His grandmother Ann didn't want him to drop out of his degree course as he had already completed his first year and been awarded a distinction, and his long-term plan was to be a graphic designer working and living in New York," Toni told nailseapeople.co.uk.

Indeed, the world of show business was a precarious one and there was no guarantee George would succeed. But at the same time, he had already come further than he could have imagined in his wildest dreams.

And so the show went on, with the stakes rising by the minute and everyone showing some kind of strain. Now that the participants had been narrowed down to the finalists, the public was taking an increasing interest in them as individuals, in their backgrounds and interests, who they really were and what they were really like.

In return, these individual personalities were beginning to influence the show. When the theme was Best of British, the boys performed 'Fix You': "This week we're dedicating our song to everyone who has fought and is fighting for our country because we feel that the armed forces are one of the best things about Britain," said George, with his Royal Marine brother, Will, very much in mind. Now that the public knew much more about him, they connected with the dedication of the award too.

Indeed, Will having served in Afghanistan garnered a lot of respect from the public. "George and Union J feel they would like to show the nation their respect for the forces on Remembrance weekend," Toni told westonsupermarepeople.co.uk. "They hope all Royal Marines, soldiers and their families will appreciate it. George has a special place in his heart for the Royal Marines as his brother is a serving Royal Marine commando." It really touched a nerve with people who were aware of the dangers brave young men like Will were facing on the front line.

By now, of course, all the contestants were garnering a huge amount of support from their home communities, who were showing their pride in 'local boys done good'. George was no different in that respect. Regional newspapers and online services were running interviews with his family, digging up old photos of him as a child and urging local people to back him – not that they needed much urging.

Students at Weston College had made a huge banner reading, 'Supporting Union J', as well as masks with George's face on it, which they wore as they held the banner aloft. Sarah Clark, Head of Faculty (Creative Arts), said: "There is a huge amount of support for George around North Somerset and we thought he and Union J deserved a boost from Weston College. We wish him and the band the best of luck."

George responded graciously: "It was stressful coming in the bottom two last weekend but we survived and we worked really hard towards this week's show – so hard, in fact, that I've got a sore throat! We've so much support around the UK, but it's essential we get our home towns and places we're connected with behind us. It's wicked that Weston College have made a banner to support us and we're really grateful to everyone for doing it."

So was the whole family. Toni and her mother visited Weston College to thank everyone in person, revealing how the whole thing had become an emotional roller coaster. "It's fantastic Union J have got through," she told assembled faculty members and students. "I can't believe it's happening sometimes, especially when I look out of our house and there are girls calling and even crying for George. He's been working around-the-clock but came home for a surprise visit and when he walked in the room it was a shock to see my son for real and not on the TV!"

Screaming girls were now present everywhere that the boys went. This was perhaps even more unreal for George than for the others, because they at least had been actively pursuing careers as pop stars. Screaming girls went with the territory of Triple J and Rewind – whereas they were not a big aspect of studying graphic design.

It takes a lot of time for most pop stars to get used to it, whereas George had none. Gossip was also constantly linking him to his stunning co-contestant Ella Henderson, which did nothing to harm his blossoming reputation as a ladies' man (as the press was beginning to dub him, not least because of his popularity with female fans). He had changed beyond all recognition from his school days.

Indeed, for a couple of people with no prior experience in dealing with the press, the two were playing a cat-and-mouse game quite brilliantly. It was said that their fellow contestants had dared them to kiss, and they were spotted holding hands.

The chemistry between them spoke volumes, yet were they an item? They wouldn't say.

They were "in synch with one another", according to Ella before they visited Disneyland Paris (with the rest of Union J), during which it was intensely speculated that Ella had transferred her attentions to Josh. In fact, she and Josh had known one another earlier in life, although no one seemed any clearer what the relationship was then either. It all served to heighten curiosity about the show, the contestants and everyone involved.

The two then proceeded to tweet pictures of themselves in Eurodisney wearing Minnie Mouse ears, but Ella seemed keen to dampen speculation about her and George in an interview with *Fabulous* magazine: "You don't come into this competition or this kind of show to make a friend for life and stuff but with certain people I think I've found that and it's really nice."

George was becoming a little overwhelmed by all the attention. It is impossible to imagine what it is like to be in the eye of the storm until it suddenly happens to you, and this 19-year-old boy now found himself part of a sensation. Something had to give.

George deleted his Instagram, which until then had been showing lots of pictures of his young self. It did absolutely nothing to dampen interest in him – if anything, the opposite was the case – and it didn't stop speculation about his love life.

"I love a lady who can make me laugh and I'm a sucker for big brown eyes," he revealed. "Demi Lovato is hot. I'd take her camping somewhere warm, like Australia, we could cook barbecues on the beach and go surfing. That would be romantic!" he told OceanUp.

(Demi was linked to Niall Horan of One Direction, something fans were not slow to point out.)

Louis fanned the flames by promising to hand over her number, and George's reputation as a ladies' man continued to grow.

Then there were all the comparisons to Harry Styles. These were not new: there was an undeniable resemblance (although, when George finally met the great man, he said that he and Harry looked totally different) and people had been telling George he looked like Harry for some time. But now, given that Union J were coming up so hot on the heels of One Direction, the implication was that he was doing it deliberately. It was a point of irritation and he was quick to deny it.

"The look I have now is the look I had three years ago," George told *The Sun*. "When One Direction came on the scene, people were saying, 'Harry Styles looks like you,' and then it started being, 'You look like Harry Styles.' [But] One Direction are so massive that it can't be anything but good to be compared to them. To have half of their success would be wicked."

And now, of course, it was beginning to look as if Union J was going to achieve just that.

George's family was awestruck. To have produced so many musicians in the past, and then to see one of the family begin to make it in such a big way, was beyond any of their dreams. That George was now visibly turning into a pop star before their very eyes was almost too much to comprehend. It wasn't just him that had to get used to the screaming girls – it was the rest of his family too. His younger sister, Harriet, still at Weston College where George had been until recently, was finding it particularly hard to comprehend the change taking place in her brother's life. But there was no going back now. Win or lose, the group had established itself via reality TV, with all of the pleasures and aggravations that would entail.

While all the attention could seem a little overwhelming, there were big advantages to it too. George was seen leaving the extremely fashionable central London nightclub Mahiki, holding hands with a mystery blonde (not Ella – it really did seem they were 'just good friends'). Girls were throwing themselves at him constantly and generally regarding him as an idol. George was fortunate in that, if he'd remained a solo singer and got through to the final, he would have had to face all of this alone. But each of the four members of the band knew how each other was feeling, providing some laddishness to bring it all back to earth.

A combination of chance, opportunity and talent had propelled an erstwhile chubby little boy who moved schools too often to bond with people into a major star. "*The X Factor* has been an amazing platform for George and a brilliant opportunity for him," Toni told Clevedonpeople.co.uk. "He has taken all of it in his stride and I am so proud of him – I just cannot put that into words. I never imagined I would be sat at home on a Saturday night watching my son singing in a prime-time talent show or performing alongside Rod Stewart. *The X Factor* has given George a lot of confidence. He said he went in as a solo performer and now cannot imagine performing without being alongside the other guys."

He was adaptable, he'd seized the challenge, gone with the moment and it was paying off brilliantly. Supporters of Team George were getting more numerous by the day.

He was also the final crucial element in Union J, which works far better as a quartet than it would have done with just three. The boys' appeal was obvious: there was a slight physical similarity between the four of them; each one would build up their own fanbase, for every Union J fan had her favourite and every member of Union J had his own individual appeal. George's multiple appeal comprised his hair, his musical abilities and the fact that it would be easy to imagine him as the boy next door. His looks are not quite as exotic as Josh's, while at the same time they were brimming with winsome appeal.

The decision not to go back to college had paid off – it had been a gamble, but the work had nowhere near stopped. In fact it had hardly even started, because it was hard work being a pop star. After the rehearsing, he would be out on the road with nowhere near as many opportunities to eat his mothers' roasts. But it was the opportunity of a lifetime and George intended to seize it with both hands.

And so to the really crucial information about George, as gleaned from *The X Factor* itself: he's never dyed his hair, washes it every day and can't live without matte wax, styling his hair by putting wax on it when it's wet and ruffling it up; his favourite high street store is River Island; his style icon is Matt Cardle and he'd always choose style over comfort; his favourite contestant for style is Jade Ellis and he thinks the best judge on the show has been Cheryl Cole. He prefers silver jewellery to gold, thinks of his own style as smart casual and thinks long hair on boys is "kinda weird". Oh, and he's got a very bright future in front of him.

The fat child who had to overcome bullying is now a major heart-throb with an internationally famous band. As they say, the best revenge is to live well.

8

Dopey Spice

If ever a place dictated the early career of one of its inhabitants, it is the market town of Newmarket, set in the Suffolk countryside about 65 miles north of London. It is the home of international horse racing, with the largest racehorse training centre and breeding centre in Britain, over 50 training stables, two large racetracks – the Rowley Mile and the July Course – and over 3,000 racehorses in the vicinity. It is also the home of the National Horseracing Museum, racehorse auctioneers Tattersalls, two equine hospitals and over 60 horse breeding studs. The Jockey Club's clubhouse is also based locally, although its administration is in London.

Newmarket's atmosphere and history could scarcely be more equine. Racing at Newmarket dates back to 1174, which means it's the earliest known racing site of post-classical times, favoured by both James I and Charles I in the 17th century, the latter of whom inaugurated the first cup race in 1634. These days, about one in three of the town's 15,000-strong population is estimated to be connected to the racing world and many of the most famous trainers in the world are based in the town, including Sir Henry Cecil, Sir Michael Soute, John Gosden, Saeed bin Suroor, Mahmood Al Zarooni and Clive Brittain. The Rowley Mile, meanwhile, plays host to two classic races – the 2,000 Guineas and 1,000 Guineas – while the July Course hosts the July Cup and Falmouth Stakes, and various other very famous races. The two courses are separated by the Devil's Dyke.

Newmarket is the place to be if your career involves horse-racing, but not necessarily where you would expect to find a member of an increasingly famous boy band. JJ Hamblett had a totally different background from the other members of Union J – Josh and Jaymi had known they wanted to be performers right from the start and George, while not professionally trained, came from a very musical background. JJ was from a more rarefied world, however, and were it not for the fact that he inconveniently grew beyond the ideal height for a jockey, the make-up of Union J might have been very different. For JJ was initially meant for a career in flat racing – before events took a very different turn.

Given Newmarket's credentials as the centre of the racing world, it was unsurprising that the jockey Paul Hamblett, who managed third place in the 1989 1,000 Guineas and second spot in the Irish equivalent, settled down in this ancient town. Paul had been a famous jockey in his day, so he and his wife, Karin, hoped that their own love of horses would pass on to the next generation. It did. First their eldest son, Ashley, became a jockey (and still is), followed by Jamie, who was born on May 25, 1988.

The brothers' little sister, Otea, appeared when Jamie had reached the grand old age of 18. He was always known as Jamie until the Rewind days, when he turned into 'JJ' to differentiate himself from Jaymi. When he was known as a jockey, however, he was Jamie Hamblett, and he had quite a bit of success under that name.

Both of the boys inherited the family love of racing and horses and decided they wanted to be jockeys when they were still very young. Both had been riding horses throughout almost their entire lives and it didn't take them long to get to the really powerful thoroughbreds. "I rode ponies when I was little and I think I sat on my first racehorse when I was 12," Ashley later told *Horse Racing* magazine. Given the circumstances, it is highly unlikely they would have become anything other than jockeys. Both boys became apprenticed at an early age to leading trainers: Ashley, aged 13, to Luca Cumani, with whom the boys' father had trained previously, and Jamie, aged 14, to Sir Michael Soute, one of the most famous trainers in the country.

Flat racing, to the uninitiated, is exactly as it sounds: it is a race on flat ground, differentiating it from steeplechasing which involves hurdles. It is a test of speed, stamina and skill, and jockeys are required to weigh as little as possible in order not to place an unduly heavy burden on the horse. It is thus in the same category as ballet, in which the body must conform to a certain type: skinny and preferably short. No matter how skilled the rider, if he (or she) gets too big for whatever reason, including growing too much, then a top-notch career as a jockey is now denied to the individual. However, most people involved in flat racing have spent their entire lives around horses and giving it up can be extremely hard. Many never break away entirely and remain in the business in some capacity, surrounded by reminders of what they have lost. Such a fate could have awaited JJ – but he managed to make the break.

But back when they were younger, both boys were as horse-mad as their father, never envisaging that a very different career might lie ahead for either of them (nor indeed that JJ would continue to grow). And so the boys took up their apprenticeships.

Despite their familiarity with the racing world, now that they were actually a part of it there was a lot to take onboard, with Ashley describing his first few visits to the weighing room as "like walking into another world". The boys' weight was to be a constant concern from now on, to be monitored strictly, catered for accordingly and obsessed about in a manner usually associated with young girls. But the pressure was there right from the start: the boys could not go beyond a certain size; if they did, all was lost.

At the start, all was going well. "I went to Mr Cumani's the following year [aged 13]," Ashley told *Horse Racing*. "Dad was his second jockey when [jockey turned trainer] Rae Guest was there and knew he was a good man with apprentices. Mr Cumani's very loyal to me – always there if I need advice or a chat."

"I was riding out for Rae Guest, but I was always saying that I wanted to move to a bigger yard," JJ chipped in. "Dad asked me who I wanted to work for, I said Sir Michael Stoute, but he thought that with me being only 14 he wouldn't want to take me on." Sir Michael did, however, and proved very helpful. "Even when I have an outside ride, he'll watch the race and have a word with me afterwards, telling me what I did right and what I did wrong. It's a great help," said JJ.

(An 'outside ride' is riding a horse from another stables, crucial for jockeys who want to make their mark in the sport.)

Sir Michael was complimentary about his protégé: "He's getting plenty of exposure on the racetrack now and he's developed a nice position in the saddle," he said affably. "He needs to work on his strength, but he's got talent and is certainly on an upward curve. I can see the progress he's making and he's the kind of rider who could end up doing well for himself."

It was important to find outside rides to build their reputation, although they were getting help from some of the biggest names in the racing world, including Frankie Dettori, Robert Winston and Kieren Fallon. Both Ashley and JJ were doing well at this stage, with seemingly great futures in the sport.

But then there was always weight to worry about. Coming from a racing family herself, this was an issue that Karin had always been aware of and so she catered for her sons accordingly. "I eat very well at home, because after feeding dad, mum knows what kind of food jockeys ought to have," Ashley told *Horse Racing*. JJ added: "I don't have to watch what I eat, but I don't eat that much anyway – I hate getting full up. I'm training myself not to put on weight!"

He spoke too soon. Tellingly, the paper reported that both boys were aware of an argument in the racing world that the permitted weight of jockeys should be raised. People were beginning to grow much taller than they used to be, not least because most people's diets were so much better than before, and it simply wasn't practical to maintain the rigid standards that once existed. Careers were being brought to an end because tall young men simply couldn't keep themselves down to skin and bone.

"A lot of apprentices are in the same boat," said JJ. "It would make life a lot easier for a lot of people if the weights were raised, although I can see the point of the lighter jockeys saying that a weight rise would take rides from them."

JJ was at the time 7st 12lb, but there were already signs that weight could be a problem. He was growing taller and his would be an almost impossible weight to maintain. It may have occurred to JJ that he might not be able to pursue the career that had done so much for his father and brother, and that he was going to have to cast around for something else to do instead.

This might have been behind another comment in the interview: "I don't set myself targets, I just hope to get more and more successful," he said, to which Ashley jumped in with, "Come on Jamie, you've got to be hungry, that's your problem."

"I am hungry, I just don't set myself targets," said JJ. "I just say to myself that one day it'll all come together."

It would, although not in the way that he expected. But his remark was very revealing. JJ has always been described as extremely likeable and also very laid-back, and one way to interpret his remark would be that he didn't have the fire in his belly needed to succeed. But in actual fact, he has succeeded in a field every bit as competitive as flat racing: show business. Unlike other jockeys who were unable to continue, he has actually forged a totally different career. It's far more likely that JJ was beginning to realise he would one day have to leave racing, and that the most sensible way to progress was not to get his hopes too high about a career that might never be his.

In actual fact though, JJ's career as a jockey was very successful: he rode in over 270 races and had 24 wins. He also met the most famous racing enthusiast in the country, if not the world. Sir Michael had trained some horses for Elizabeth II and JJ had ridden some of them too. Occasionally, the monarch would come to the stables to see for herself that all was well.

"Having ridden for the Queen, I was lucky enough to meet her," JJ told the *Daily Express*. "Once or twice a year, she would pop into the yard to check on her horses – it was so weird seeing her. She sauntered in wearing Wellington boots as if it was normal – and she walked into the horses' box that I was in at the time. She said 'hello', fed the horses grass and left. Apart from *The X Factor*, it was the most surreal moment of my life."

Both boys were encouraged by their father who, having retired from racing, was now working as a mobile cleaner and was delighted they were taking to the family profession so well. Indeed, he positively commanded them to get on with it.

"He keeps asking why haven't you got a ride today, phone your agent and ask why you don't have a ride," Jamie told *Horse Racing* in an interview during his jockeying days. "Then he tells us to go for a run or something, to get us out of the house."

It was a very active, sporty existence. The boys were young, keen and bursting with energy, and the path ahead seemed clear. As an adult, JJ told one interviewer that in many ways he preferred horses to people, given that they were less complicated; it cannot be overstated, however, how much people like JJ, who is also uncomplicated and inspires affection and loyalty wherever he goes.

For his schooling, JJ attended Soham Village College, followed by Scaltback Middle School. The first of these was a very prestigious establishment, dating from 1686, with the building in which it was housed from 1925 belonging to Newmarket jockey Charles Morbey. The second was a pleasant seat of learning founded in 1972. It is fair to say that JJ was not a particularly academic boy, but he was as popular at school as he was to become everywhere else. Even as a child he enjoyed music, with Backstreet Boys as his favourite band.

However, much as he loved racing, JJ was beginning to have a problem with keeping his weight down. He was growing into a tall young man and, under natural circumstances, would have been at the very least 10 stone, which would still make him very slim for his height. But jockeys are not allowed to weigh more than eight stone.

And so a long period of transition began. JJ continued to work with horses – after all, they had been his entire life so far – but also started to look further afield for other opportunities. It wasn't easy. JJ came from a horsey family and the world of racing is both an enclosed and an intoxicating one. It is not easy to break free and make a career elsewhere. But for all the teasing JJ takes about being a bit of a dreamer, no one could accuse him of lacking ambition or determination.

He had one famous precedent – Davy Jones had been apprenticed to Newmarket trainer Basil Foster before he, too, left to join a boy band, The Monkees. Not that JJ had any idea that would be his future – he had his mind on other things first.

JJ may have been growing too tall to be a jockey, but his changing appearance began to offer up other opportunities. He was growing into his looks. JJ had never been plump, like George – quite the opposite, in fact – but while George had to lose weight to achieve his potential, JJ had to gain it.

Although by any normal standards JJ was remarkably slim, he began to fill out just enough to look really striking. Cheekbones appeared on his classically symmetrical face: a straight nose, large dark eyes and attractive olive skin. There was plenty of dark brown hair – nearly black – that could be teased up into a quiff. And so it began to occur to JJ that perhaps he would make a career out of the fact he was becoming strikingly handsome.

JJ decided that modelling and acting were the future and signed up with the online agency StarNow, at which point he started getting picked for the odd photo shoot or audition. He even got the odd small part of the blink-and-you'll-miss-it variety, although the productions he appeared in were not particularly prestigious. But he began to make his mark in a very small way. His CV is still on the site, along with a number of modelling shots:

I am a very hard worker and a professional at what i have done, i have got the drive to make a name for myself as an actor and believe i have the ability to do so. 'Success is not final, failure is not fatal: it is the courage to continue that counts.'

JJ listed himself under both the modelling and acting sections. As a model, he wrote that he was just starting out and had little experience, but as an actor he had begun to get somewhere. His entry reads as follows (the capitals and grammatical structure are his):

> I have been trying to pursue My Acting Career for a year now which I have had a great deal of luck with what I have gone for! My first Audition was for the BBC series *The Cut* which for me was great, of this the director said he liked me but was looking for someone slightly different for the role! This gave me a great experience for my up coming auditions.
>
> My Second audition was For a Low Budget Feature film Called *Vampires Don't Cry*, In this I had to play a 15-year-old School boy. I had to play childish and young to portray this role.

Vampires Don't Cry, which was filmed in 2009, was described as "five ancient but eternally youthful and beautiful female vampires living in Modern day London. Think *Sex & The City* meets *Interview With The Vampire*." It was not a major commercial success.

> Lastly I went to an audition for Campus 202 this was a University series about a Campus of which there was murders and Drugs involved, In this I played 'Fredrico' he was a 18-year-old student, he was a quiet, sly inner city

person from London which he was heavily involved in supplying drugs to the other students on campus! I really try to base myself as an Versatile Actor and try to play different and unusual characters. Although the series and feature film were not made successful and I have not been acting long I think I have gained massive experience In what I have achieved over the past year and I am looking to be put into the right direction and given a chance.

He was about to be given it – and then some. But for all this time he remained involved in the equestrian world, right up through the Rewind days until *The X Factor* came along. He was not earning enough money from his new way of life to support himself, and in any case he loved his horses and his friends. His family and his way of life were all situated in Newmarket. The final break had not been made yet.

9

Fast Forward

JJ Hamblett had by now grown into a tall, handsome man. Well before he joined a band or appeared on *The X Factor*, he was extremely popular with the girls. He attracted them effortlessly and, while he had girlfriends, he was also happy to play the field. His laid-back demeanour and happy-go-lucky attitude proved hugely attractive and JJ would often find women buzzing around him like flies. This was also an early indication that he was exactly the sort of person who would succeed in a boy band. Indeed, around this time he started performing occasionally with bands, gaining a little experience before he joined Rewind.

Towards the end of his career in racing, JJ went to work for trainer John Gosden at Clarehaven Stables in Bury Road, Newmarket, having previously worked at the next-door stables and knowing a lot of people in the yard. While he was very popular with his fellow jockeys, by now it was known that he was pursuing a career outside of racing and he had to take some stick from the others – for example, being called 'pretty boy' when he started his career in modelling. It was all part of the banter of the yard, which everyone engaged in and JJ took in good part. He kept his stablemates informed when he joined Rewind – which they promptly dubbed 'Fast Forward' – and worried constantly about upsetting the schedule when he took time off for auditions. He also showed his colleagues footage of Rewind's first ever performance and – although they never let up on the teasing – they were immensely proud of their talented protégé.

It was while working part-time for Gosden, and trying to build a career in acting, modelling and music, that Jamie attracted the attention of Kasey Monroe, who had seen some of his publicity shots. She immediately realised this was just the sort of person she and Julian White were looking for: young, fresh faced, brimming with charm and enthusiasm, JJ looked like the perfect fit for her new boy band. He also had a small amount of musical experience by that point, enough to hint at a new career. And so began its first momentous stages.

As we have seen earlier, after several stops and starts and changes of heart, the five-piece that was eventually to be called Rewind fell into place. JJ and Josh Thomas soon became firm friends, but while Josh had already had some experience in the business, JJ's was negligible. As well as having to hone his singing and dancing techniques, he also had to start learning about the music business – and fast.

JJ was still working with horses, so life was becoming increasingly complicated. He was commuting between Newmarket and Surrey where the band was working, fitting in rehearsals around his job and simply trying to get used to his new life. Just a few years earlier, when he bumped into the Queen in the stable yard, he can scarcely have anticipated that riding her horses would be a prelude to one day appearing before her onstage.

If it hadn't been the future he had previously envisaged, it was still looking promising all the same. At that stage, Rewind, still as yet unnamed, was being talked of as following in the steps of JLS.

"Kasey got hold of me after seeing my pictures and asked me if I could sing," JJ told the *Mirror* in a very early interview, when a buzz was beginning to build up about the band. Julian let it be known that he had a major new talent on his hands and people were beginning to express an interest in meeting the boys.

"I put something on YouTube for [Kasey] and it went from there," said JJ. "Kasey basically went on image at first, but we all met up for the first time earlier this month and it went really well. With Westlife finishing next year, there will be a gap for a new boy band that needs filling and we want to be the ones to do that."

He also touched on a theme he would frequently revert to in interviews to come: "I haven't got a girlfriend, but hopefully that will come." Suffice to say, there was no shortage of contenders for the role.

Julian also contributed to the piece:

> The band has been put together, the songs have been written and we are ready to record. Once they are recorded we will go round the record labels. Two major labels already know what I'm doing and they're keeping a close eye on it. The name of the band should always come from the members themselves and, once that has been sorted and the recordings are done, we will start a full-frontal attack on the labels.

That particular scenario did not work out as planned. But in those early days, everything simply looked positive and there was still everything to play for. Excitement was mounting as the boys started to realise that it really could happen.

"We all chose names and mine was picked," says Julian. "Rewind: Billy Humphreys designed the logo." Julian also solicited an early interview for the boys in the *Racing Post*, on the basis of JJ's former career as a jockey.

At this point JJ formed an extremely close bond with Kasey. "JJ and I were friends," she recalls, "not just manager and artist. He called me every day, didn't miss one day, even just to say 'hi' and ask how I was. He was sweet that way. None of the rest of them would have ever thought to do that. I also came up with the name JJ, and he told me, 'I don't want to be called JJ, I hate it.' I said, 'Well, that is what you are called,' only because I kept getting them all mixed up and it was driving me mad. No one actually called him it until he was on *X Factor* and they said JJ – and I realised they were using the name I made for him, the one he hated."

It was a sad way for the friendship to end. But in the interim, JJ became the oldest member of Union J, as the band was now to be called, and was given the nickname 'Dopey Spice' to tease him, as he is sometimes a little slow. This is at odds with the wearing of large, black-rimmed glasses which give him a some-what studious air. In actual fact, JJ has a slightly dreamy personal-ity; the boys say that he has always got his head in the clouds or acts like he's on a different planet. Sometimes it takes him a little longer than the others to get a joke, and it's perhaps ironic that for some time his ringtone was 'Wide Awake' by Katy Perry. But he has a genuinely sweet nature that is not a given in show business circles, a generosity of spirit that sets him apart. While he might not be a great intellectual, he was hard working, deter-mined and ambitious enough to know that he wanted to be famous.

But he didn't rub people up the wrong way in the pursuit of fame. It is impossible to find anyone with a bad word to say about him, and he proved as popular in his new life as he had been as a jockey in his old: utterly calm, relaxed, easy-going and, above all, kind. It was telling that, when Union J were interviewed by Digital Spy, they were asked which band member they would go out with if they were a girl. Both Josh and George chose JJ, the former on the grounds that he was "down to earth" and the latter "because you can walk all over him". (JJ, incidentally, chose George because "he's a nice, sweet guy".) But it wasn't really a question of walking over anyone – JJ was just so good natured that he was never confrontational, never got into fights with anyone and was totally content to take life as it came. It was thus all the more incongruous that he ended up in the middle of the upset caused by Rewind morphing into Triple J, as he would have hated all the bad feeling. But life, as he had already learned, does not always go according to plan.

★   ★   ★

By the time the move was made to Blair Dreelan's management, the boys also knew they were going to try for *The X Factor*, something that was exciting and terrifying all at once. Just like the rest of the band, JJ was going to have to do his growing up in public, learning his trade with the entire country tuning in to watch him. JJ had been in the odd boy band before Rewind, but nothing serious had come of it; even in Rewind itself, rehearsals had always been pretty desultory. He had never done anything like what was required of him now.

JJ had had a little more experience than George of performing in front of an audience, but not much. "Previously I had only ever sung in front of about 50 people, so to suddenly be singing in front of 8,000 people at the O2 was amazing," he told the *Newmarket Journal*. "I have always loved singing but never had the bottle. When I stopped race riding it gave me the drive to do something else. When I was 22 I was in a couple of failed singing projects and did a bit of acting stuff, but nothing really took off. The three of us started this project and decided we should go for *The X Factor*. Singing is something I've always wanted to do and I'm grateful that I'm doing something that I've always wanted to do."

For a novice at public performance, JJ pulled off a remarkable feat. Famously, a couple of years earlier, when One Direction was in the same position, Harry Styles would become so ill with nerves that he would be sick before he went onstage. JJ, in contrast, could scarcely have been more relaxed. This is when his easy-going personality came into its own; he looked as if he'd been performing all his life, not as if he was a member of a very recently formed boy band that had only had a few rehearsals. His calm and soothing personality could not have been a better antidote to the hysterical atmosphere of *The X Factor*: as the audience screamed, shouted, cheered or worked themselves into a frenzy, JJ just smiled and took it all in his stride. He seemed totally unfazed by all the attention – although, of course, as the series wore on, he wanted to win as badly as everyone else.

As with the other members of Union J, JJ's family was providing limitless support. Karin and Otea were regularly travelling up to London to watch him on the show; Ashley was tweeting, telling everyone to vote for Union J and Paul was going one step further, teaming up with the *Newmarket Journal* to hand out flyers urging people to support his son. He was delighted that, even if JJ wasn't going to have a career in racing, he looked likely to do well elsewhere. His father, as much as anyone, knew how level headed JJ was and so there were no worries about letting his son loose in the bright lights, big city world of show business. JJ was in his twenties now and perfectly able to look after himself.

"About 175,000 people started the *X Factor* journey and Union J is now one of the final seven," Paul told the paper. "We want to get posters in as many shops as we can in Newmarket to give the band the support that they deserve. It's something you only dream about. Jamie has always been ambitious and he was always singing as a boy. Words can't describe how we would feel if they were to win the competition. It's something that they want badly. You could see that by how devastated they were when they were in the bottom two. We would never have stood in the way of it because he's always had his feet firmly on the ground. He has got a heart of gold."

While JJ had not attracted quite the same amount of press as his bandmates, possibly because of his very laid-back demeanour, he was now attracting huge amounts of attention from the girls. The audience loved him and there was widespread delight when (often topless) pictures of him from his modelling days emerged. Looking slender as a willow, he gave a very good illustration as to how feather-light a jockey had to be.

Each series of *The X Factor* throws up dozens of additional stories in its wake, and this one was no different. First there was George, with his intensively musical background and now there was horse-mad JJ, who had initially wanted to be a jockey. Neither was exactly what the audience expected, but both were hugely popular.

At first JJ's friends and former colleagues from the racing world reacted with astonishment at his new career. It was no secret that he'd been trying to make it as a model and actor, and more latterly as a singer, but it is one thing to know your acquaintance is trying to break into the world of show business and quite another to see him plastered all over the nation's plasma screens, looking so relaxed and confident. The racing world, so very much more down to earth, was bemused.

"It's strange seeing someone you ride out with every morning appearing on TV on something like *The X Factor*," jockey Nicky Mackay told lovetheraces.com. "But fair play to him, he's done really well and is up there now with a really good chance on a programme which opens up plenty of doors. I mean look at One Direction – they didn't even win it! It takes a lot of guts to try your hand at something completely different. I'm not sure there's ever been anyone famous from Newmarket from outside of racing and this shows that it isn't necessarily the be-all and end-all of success!"

Fellow jockey and friend Kirsty Milczarek felt the same, well aware that JJ had been very lucky to find an alternative career. "It's nice that he's got a career outside of racing, because a lot of people get stuck in a rut when being a jockey doesn't work out for you," she told ITV. "You end up riding out for years and years and years. It's nice he's got an interest outside of racing and I wish him all the best," she said – adding that fellow jockey Fergus Sweeney was pretty talented, and perhaps he should think about *The X Factor*, too.

In some ways, JJ's change of career made a lot of sense. Horse racing, which can be a dangerous sport, produces a lot of adrenaline, especially when the jockey wins – which JJ had done on numerous occasions by then. When people leave racing they miss that huge surge of adrenaline, which is difficult to replicate elsewhere. But it's also obtained by performing in front of a huge audience. One of the reasons that JJ always appears so calm, when the crowd is going wild, is that he has experienced that rush to the head before.

As the series wore on, it became apparent there were other added attractions. JJ was very taken by one of the backing dancers, a Brazilian beauty by the name of Rithiely 'Rithy' Pereira, and it wasn't long before the two had become a couple behind the scenes. "JJ couldn't keep his eyes off Rithy the first time he spotted her backstage at *The X Factor*," a source on the show told *The Sun*. "They started chatting and she agreed to go out with him for a date. Now he's really into her."

Rithy was an exotic creature. Originally from Sao Paulo, she moved at the age of 10 to Zurich, where her mother had already emigrated; when JJ met her, she was assistant director at the American School of Dance, teaching a group called ID8 and managing another group called Legacy. She was well aware of the pressures of JJ's new world, having worked as a dancer on the Natalia Meets Anastacia tour as well as appearing on the BBC's *So You Think You Can Dance*.

Rithy and JJ did not make a big song and dance about their relationship. It was early days and everything had to be played out in the public eye. Rithy was also a TV veteran and knew there were occasions when it was better to keep everyone guessing. This was very much the case now.

At Christmas, JJ headed back to Newmarket for a short break with his family and to catch up with his old friends in the racing world. Indeed, just like George and his friends at Weston College, who were so keen to support him, JJ's racing colleagues were very proud of what he had achieved. They noted with approval that he was as down to earth as ever, and that his growing fame had not gone to his head. But then, it was never likely to.

JJ was so solidly well-grounded that, even faced with the kind of fame and adulation which would have swept many a young man off his feet, he still managed to stay unfazed. His tweets from that period reinforce the point: he tweeted happily about

McDonald's and Indian food; about watching *Only Fools &
Horses*; about having a hot bath and failing to do his Christmas
shopping. It was all harmless, laddish stuff that might have come
from any young man about town, rather than a major star.

JJ's generous spirit showed in plenty of ways, not least his
willingness to engage as much as he could with the local community – he was one of their own, after all. He delighted
children at Fordham Primary School, where his seven-year-old
sister, Otea, was a pupil, by turning up for a meet and greet.

"It's amazing to come back to my sister's school and see all the
little kids and the families," he told the *Newmarket Journal*. "I am
quite close to the people in Fordham so it's just nice to see the
reaction when I come back to school. It makes it more real and
it's really humbling."

Otea herself was thrilled: "My friends keep coming up to me
saying, 'When is he coming to school to sing?'" Not only did
she have a famous pop star as a brother, but he even turned up to
meet all of her friends.

When the show was over, tension was mounting about what
was going to happen next. A record deal was obviously on the
cards, but even the usually imperturbable JJ was a little anxious
to get it wrapped up. And he was finding the experience as
surreal as everyone else. "We're so excited to see what's going
to happen," JJ told the *Newmarket Journal*. "We want to get
signed, we want to make an album and get touring Britain so we
can build our fanbase."

His father, Paul, was also relieved that a contract with Sony
was being signed. "They are crossing the T's and dotting the I's
at the moment," he said. "They have some shows coming up,
but hopefully they are going to sign in the next few days. It
is going to be big. It's nice to know they aren't left high and

dry, which a lot of groups often are. They are making their way."

Indeed, that always was the danger with these shows. Many acts were signed, or promised a contract that never materialised, and Josh had already been with various bands that had failed to take off. But it was almost inconceivable that it would happen now. Industry insiders were increasingly certain that Union J had as bright a future as One Direction. It was only a case of sorting out the details.

In JJ's case, it really couldn't have happened to a nicer guy. More facts began to emerge about this new heart-throb: JJ's favourite film is *I Love You Man*; he is a fan of Justin Bieber and has a tattoo of an angel playing cards on his left arm; he is one quarter Norwegian; his star sign is Gemini; he is 5′ 10″ (too tall for a jockey) and weighs 138lbs; he sleepwalks, talking in his sleep as he does, and has an irrational fear of rubber bands; his shoe size is 6.5 – and he is destined for greater things.

10

Bossy Spice

November 2012.

A member of one of the biggest up and coming bands in show business was about to take the gamble of his career. Jaymi Hensley, a member of new teen sensation Union J and a heart-throb to millions of girls, had just learned that a newspaper had caught wind of the fact he was gay and was preparing to put the story on the front page.

Attitudes to homosexuality had changed beyond all recognition in recent decades, with many big names in show business making no secret of their predilections. But there remained two areas where it was seen as a problem: Hollywood stars and teen heart-throbs. There is still no openly gay major Hollywood star (although there are plenty of rumours about who ought to be), while the whole point of a teen heart-throb is that girls can fantasise about him. And that supposedly doesn't work if the star in question is gay.

With all that said, things were beginning to change. In previous years, coming out as gay could have been career suicide for a potential heart-throb – but now, society was not only more liberal than it used to be, it also accepted that people wanted to live in a way that was natural to themselves. Many people in previous generations endured a good deal of unhappiness when they were forced to hide their true inclinations, with a choice of either risking their career or being accused of hypocrisy if it ever did come out.

Ever since Will Young had come out over 10 years previously, attitudes had been changing – so much so that it was now quite possible for boy bands to have at least one openly gay member, including Stephen Gately of Boyzone, Mark Feehily of Westlife and Lance Bass of 'N SYNC. Louis Walsh, who was also gay, had managed both Westlife and Boyzone, and was clearly the right person to help Jaymi at what could have been a difficult time.

If his hand had been forced by the knowledge that a newspaper was preparing to out him, so much the better if he managed the situation on his own terms. In the end it was decided that the best policy would be to give an interview to *The Sun*. Not that long ago, *The Sun* would have been the first to carry it as a big news story in scandalous style, as it had done with Elton John in the eighties – although it turned out that the public was more than prepared to accept Elton as gay. But if one of the most popular papers in the country was onside, it was a fair bet that it could carry its readership and the rest of the country along with it.

And so the interview went ahead, revealing not only that Jaymi was gay but that he was in a long-term serious relationship (with Olly Marmon, although he didn't reveal the name of his partner at the time). Despite the changing times, it had still been a brave decision to make. As well as the risk of alienating female fans (which didn't happen, in the event), there were still plenty of people out there who were willing to pile on the homophobic abuse – it had happened to other stars, after all. But Jaymi took a deep breath and went ahead.

"I spoke to Louis about this and he said, 'Put it this way, both of my big boy bands had a gay member in them.' So he said it fits the formula quite well!" Jaymi began. "Every boy band has got to have a gay one! And Louis just said, 'Do it.' I'm gay and I've never been happier!"

It made an enormous difference, of course, that Louis was so supportive. Without his help, or with a manager whose inclination was to hide the truth, matters could have been very different.

The other members of Union J were totally supportive. Like everyone else involved, they thought it was quite right that Jamie should come out now. "They have always supported me with doing this," Jaymi continued. "I didn't want to do it in five years' time when I have made money and had a career. I don't think anyone should have to hide who they are. I'd love my career to take off to the heights of One Direction. But not enough people in the music industry are open about their sexuality." He was certainly right there.

Jaymi went on to reveal he had been in a relationship for three years, although he wasn't prepared to reveal who the other man was other than to say he was a hairdresser. "I came on to the show not wanting to be judged for my personal life," he continued. "But people have caught wind of it and I just wanted to set the record straight. It is not a big thing for me – I came out when I was 14 to my family and friends and never had one piece of negativity . . . I hope the reaction will hopefully be, 'OK, we kind of knew, but well done on coming out.' I don't want people to think I have hidden this to gain votes because I am so proud of who I am. I hope people respect me for being honest."

They did. There was not a whiff of criticism from any quarter, nor did anyone think he'd been hiding anything to gain votes from viewers. People just understood that, even in these tolerant times, it can be difficult for someone in the public eye to stand up and say that they're gay.

It also helped that Jaymi was not the only gay contestant on *The X Factor* that year – Rylan Clark, Lucy Spraggan and Jade Ellis had all been totally open about their sexuality. But what finally prompted him to follow their example was that a young fan had been in touch to ask him if it was true. It struck him at that point that Union J were not just heart-throbs: like everyone in the public eye, they had the possibility of turning into role models and even changing public opinion on matters like this. Jaymi would never have considered it before coming on the show, but the fact is that if he was personally able to make a difference for the better, then that was something he wanted to do.

"I got a tweet from a boy who must have been 13 or 14 asking if the rumours that I was gay were true," Jaymi said. "He said he really wished I could be out because he didn't have anyone to look up to and was finding it really hard to fit in and tell his parents. I was that kid at 14 and really wish I had someone to say it was OK to be pictured on the red carpet with a guy and be gay in a boy band. *The X Factor* is such a great show to show that – you've got such a great range of characters, especially Rylan who is so open. It was like if he can do it, why can't I? But I'm not going to suddenly come out and do a flamboyant performance – that's Rylan's bag."

There was another reason, too. Now that he was in the public eye, Jaymi was getting photographed everywhere he went; like so many people in his position, it was often hinted that, if he was pictured with a girl, then the chances were they were in a relationship.

"I got papped with six girls from Take Me Out," Jaymi said rather ruefully. "I woke up to my boyfriend ringing me saying,

'I'm not being funny but what did you do in the club last night?'"

Absolutely nothing that would alarm Olly, of course. But if he wanted to avoid upsetting his boyfriend and allowing false rumours to circulate, then it was time to come out.

Events proved he was right to do so. There was no backlash, no dip in popularity, no hint that matters couldn't continue as they had been – in short, no problems whatsoever. Jaymi had just become the latest member of a boy band to admit he was gay. And the world's reaction? It shrugged and said, so what?

Rylan Clark, meanwhile, said that he was delighted, and that the two would soon be painting the town pink. "I've got a lot of time for Jaymi," he said. "Nothing's changed for him – the only thing that's changed is people now know he's gay. I'm sure I'll be taking him out very soon."

There was also public support from Sir Ian McKellen, most famous to Jaymi's fanbase for playing the wizard Gandalf in *The Lord Of The Rings*. "It takes a lot of determination to decide you're going to do it," he said. "Jaymi can get on with his life and fans don't give a toss." Although he was both a gay actor and a gay rights campaigner, even Sir Ian hadn't come out until well into adulthood. But then he really had come from a different era, born at a time when practising homosexuality was still illegal. Sir Ian knew how difficult it could be to come out with something so personal in the full public glare.

If the truth be told, there had never been too much doubt about Jaymi's sexuality anyway. It had not been hidden in the Rewind days – indeed, the boys gave an interview to *Bent* magazine in which Jaymi was subject to some teasing about it – and if it had been an issue at all in Triple J or Union J, that is only because everything had happened so fast that no one had any time to think anything through. Sure, they were being marketed as teen heart-throbs, but there was no actual attempt to conceal the fact that Jaymi was gay.

It was more a case of when to come out with it and how much detail to go into. Jaymi was also going to have to decide if he wanted to name Olly or not. In the end he wasn't given too much choice, as the information was bound to become public, but then every star, gay or straight, has to decide where to draw the line between private and public lives.

Ironically, Jaymi in many ways had a more conventional set-up than the others. He alone was in a long-term relationship with a stable partner who, he was later to declare, he wanted to marry. As he was also later to say of himself, he lived a pretty typical 2.4 children lifestyle – it was just that it happened to be with another man.

★ ★ ★

James William 'Jaymi' Hensley was born on February 24, 1990, in Stopsley, Luton to Jackie and David. "If Jaymi had been a girl, he would have been called Amber," his mother once revealed. Five years later, his brother Aaron arrived. The family lived in a small, suburban area, the skyline dominated by Jansel House, an office block built in 1961, with a parade of shops, banks, estate agents, restaurants and takeaways clustered around the centre. The immediately surrounding area contained schools, one of Luton's two cemeteries, Luton Museum and Art Gallery, Luton Hoo and attractive parts of the nearby countryside, including Dunstable Downs and the Chiltern Hills. London was within easy reach when the family wanted to see the bright lights of the big city, as they would when Jaymi eventually made it his home.

Jaymi, who was to become known as 'Bossy Spice' to his

bandmates and also 'Mother', on the grounds that he made sure they got up in the morning and generally fussed that everything was as it should be, came from a very different background to George and JJ. Unlike them, he knew from a very young age that he wanted to be an entertainer. While all three of the other boys had outside jobs in totally different areas before becoming full-time performers, Jaymi's entire life was in show business. His part-time work was as a song and dance teacher and he also had various shots at a career in show business, well before the Rewind days.

For someone who was to become quite a flamboyant character, however, it was a strikingly ordinary suburban background. Jaymi attended Putteridge Primary and High Schools; the high school was a comprehensive, taking pupils from 11 to 16 for their GCSEs, and specialised in mathematics and computing. The school would express support when it realised that one of its own was appearing in *The X Factor*, but in fact Union J was Jaymi's second shot at the big time (of which more anon).

Jaymi also attended the BRIT School (real name: the London School for Performing Arts and Technology) at Selhurst, Croydon, in the south London suburbs. As its name implies, it was built to provide education and vocational training in the performing arts, with a long list of famous alumni including Katy B, Adele, Amy Winehouse, Jessie J, Leona Lewis, Katie Melua, the Kooks and Kate Nash. It was the perfect place for someone with musical talent who wanted to pursue a career as a performer, and Jaymi was in his element.

Right from the start, Jaymi's life was dominated by performance. He joined a local amateur dramatics group called the Phoenix Players and took part in musicals, including *Bye Bye Birdie*. "He was quite short and fat in that," his mother recalled.

Indeed, pictures from that time reveal a plump little boy, although, like George, he was to shed the puppy fat and grow into his looks. He appears fresh faced and excited at the point where he was first developing his singing voice.

Jaymi was becoming increasingly aware that this was not just a hobby – he wanted to pursue a career in entertainment, and so he enrolled to train at the famous Sylvia Young Theatre School in London on Saturdays. Founded in 1981, Sylvia Young has been the alma mater to some of the most famous young names in British show business, including Amy Winehouse (again), Denise Van Outen, Billie Piper, former Spice Girl Emma Bunton, *I Am Number Four* star Alex Pettyfer, Kara Tointon (Dawn from *EastEnders*), Lacey Turner (Stacey from *EastEnders*), Chenelle Olaiya, McFly member Tom Fletcher, ex Busted bass player Matt Willis, Vanessa White of The Saturdays and Nathan Sykes of The Wanted. The film *High School Musical 3* features an SYTS pupil, Jemma McKenzie-Brown. Josh was there around the same time, although the two boys didn't know each other back then. But it was the perfect place for two such ambitious young men: Jaymi studied dance, jazz and 'Singing with Bobby' – vocal instructor Bobby Pearce, who remembers both of them as "great young guys who had potential".

Sylvia Young remembers them, too. "They were popular, very pleasant nice guys," she says. "I thought they would do well, but they need opportunity as well as talent. I think they will do great stuff." She remembers both of them hanging out with other students, having coffee with the girls and learning their trade, spending two to three years in situ before moving on.

As stated previously, Jaymi had always known he was gay and, at the age of 14, came out to his parents, who were very supportive. It was never really a secret, and Jaymi's friends and family reacted much as the public was to do some years later – with total acceptance and tolerance. Although there was one small quirk: "Jaymi's celebrity crush was Beyoncé," his mother revealed.

After finishing his education, Jaymi knew he wanted a career in entertainment but was also aware that it was a very tough world out there. Needing to find some steadier work, he worked part time as a singing and dancing teacher in Luton, as well as touring as a solo singer at events including the Gran Canaria Gay Pride festival (illustrating how his gayness has never really been an issue – footage of Jaymi singing at the event still exists on the internet). He even had a very slight success with the recording of 'I Breathe Again'. He was touring, performing and making as many contacts as possible, but he still didn't quite receive that final push. Even at that early stage though, he knew that the best way to step from obscurity to fame was a reality TV show, and that the best one to appear on was *The X Factor*. So he applied to the show, got through to the finals of the Open Mic part of the competition – and then failed.

If ever a story illustrates the importance of not giving up at the first hurdle, it is Jaymi's. To say he picked himself up and started all over again would be an understatement. He continued teaching, along with any gigs he could get booked into, and the following year, aged 21, he was back at *The X Factor* – this time in a slightly different guise.

By now Jaymi had joined forces with Brock, 25, Lee Wilby, 22 and Billy Ashley, 24, in a boy band called Brooklyn, which had some initial success on the show. They at least managed to attract the attention of their local paper, *Bedford Today*: "We have been rehearsing loads, and we've been in the studio working with a guy who wrote songs for Peter Andre and The

Saturdays," Billy told the paper. "On Sunday we're going to sing 'Kiss From A Rose'. It's a slower song but we wanted to show off our vocals. I think we're the only boy band in our category so hopefully that will give us an advantage."

In the event, the boys managed to make it through the first round to audition in front of Gary Barlow, Kelly Rowland, Louis Walsh and Tulisa Contostavlos in Cardiff, in front of a massive audience – something that neither George nor JJ would experience until their own first appearances a couple of years later. One of them, at least, found it a terrifying experience.

"I have never felt that nervous before, ever," said Billy. "We were there from 6 a.m. queuing up for six hours. We'd never performed onstage before, until then we'd just rehearsed in J's bedroom, but there we were at Cardiff Arena in front of 4,000 people. My heart was racing."

But the impetus behind the band was not dissimilar to that which would drive Union J: One Direction had already shown what a boy band could do if they put their mind to it and Brooklyn was going to have a go. "Our sound is quite pop, it's similar to JLS, One Direction and The Wanted," Billy continued. "As we develop we'll probably do more of a mix of stuff. We are an all-singing, all-dancing boy band and I am proud to say that."

Despite having nearly been through the mill once, Jaymi was pretty overwhelmed as well:

> The whole experience was just surreal. We spent 24 hours a day with cameras following us round. The press were everywhere and we were being driven round in big *X Factor* buses that had to go on huge detours because we were being followed by paparazzi. When I went out back home it felt weird not having cameras everywhere, like I'd forgotten what normal life was like. You get so used to the

X Factor bubble, it's crazy. At the moment we're doing a schools tour and we'd love to visit as many as possible. *The X Factor* was a brilliant experience and we're hoping people will get to know us from that. We'd absolutely love to switch on the Christmas lights in Luton this year.

Jaymi had already worked out that *The X Factor* could be a launch pad, whether or not you actually won the competition – something that he would later comprehensively prove with Union J.

For a short time, however, Brooklyn seemed to be where it was at. The boys did their best to get noticed; they didn't have any management at that point, but would book their own gigs and run their own show.

All the same, Brooklyn did not take off in the longer term. But it gave Jaymi invaluable experience for what was to happen next.

11

Stage School Boy

By the time Jaymi was with Rewind he'd already met Olly, who had been working in a bar when Jaymi walked in – although he was now a hairdresser. He was quietly supportive in the background, and as delighted as anyone when Jaymi joined the boy band. It was a promising set-up: although there were odd tensions, the boys did acquire proper management – although at this stage Jaymi was still working part time in Luton. He was also beginning to acquire quite a major collection of tattoos, which tended to be hidden when the band were being 'styled'.

Jaymi's time with Rewind was not without hiccups. Having a lot more experience than some of the others, as well as a stage school education, Jaymi often had strong opinions about what he wanted to do and some lively discussions would ensue.

Billy Ashley, from Brooklyn, was also in Rewind and the two of them established a firm friendship. Nor was there any attempt to conceal Jaymi's homosexuality – in particular, there was the feature in *Bent* magazine. "I'd like to be on all the clubs' VIP lists, turn up with all my mates, drink as much as possible, and party till I drop, then wake up each morning feeling a new man . . . !" Jaymi told the magazine.

"Jay, you do all that already – lol," Billy replied.

All the boys had their say. "We love all our fans no matter what colour, race or creed they are," said Billy. "It is them that help us achieve our dreams and buy our records, we are nothing without them. Although it is weird when people call us sex symbols, it makes me laugh, as at school I was the geek who sat in the corner that no-one paid any attention to, the furthest thing from a sex symbol . . . Now I have fans outside my house watching my mum hang out my undies . . . one of them even stole a pair off the line – lol."

As for Josh: "I admire my nan, I am just gutted when she died last year. She struggled as a single mum to raise a family and we had nothing. She could always sing, and I grew up listening to her sing to us as kids. She always taught me to be humble and take every chance you get as things happen for a reason . . . so if she is looking down I am grabbing this chance with both hands Nan."

And JJ? "People have always scared me a bit, you see – they're so complicated. I suppose that's why I prefer horses."

Giving an interview to a gay magazine should not come as a surprise. There was one major precedent: Take That had built up a following by touring gay clubs before becoming famous and, indeed, a lot of boy bands have gay fanbases – as do many mainstream entertainers, who cultivate these fanbases by turning up at events like Gay Pride. (It was not just because of Jaymi that Union J would appear at G-A-Y nightclub – so, after all, has Kylie Minogue.)

And then of course came the split, and the formation of Union J. Sadly, there was some bad feeling and Jaymi's friendship with Billy did not survive.

* * *

Given that he'd already been around for some time now, with two cracks at *The X Factor* under his belt, Jaymi was as astonished as the other boys when, in their new incarnation, they began to take off. His old school and the local community got wildly overexcited when they realised that one of their own was on *The X Factor*, and began to drum up support. As with all the other members of Union J, his family were the first to lead the way and were happy to talk to the local press. "It's surreal and just hasn't sunk in at all," Jaymi's brother Aaron, then 17, said on the Luton Sixth Form College website. "We've spent the last few days putting banners and posters up all over Luton – we've been putting them up in the Arndale and in Stopsley village, where my mum works at Henderson's Newsagents. I'm looking forward to it and I reckon they've got a good chance – they've got a good fanbase already. Jaymi's tried for *X Factor* before and has reached the final of the Open Mic UK competition and sung at the O2 – it feels like his hard work has finally paid off."

He was certainly beginning to live the dream. Like the others, girls were screaming at him and trying to get near him. Although he had not yet come out to *The Sun*, it was his personal appeal, celebrity and talent that they were responding to. But at that stage it was all so new and so unexpected that Jaymi was as taken aback as everyone else.

It was third time lucky. After several different tries at stardom, he'd finally clicked with the right combination of people. "I had a girl faint in my arms on Sunday," he told Heatworld.com as the madness really started. "I didn't know what to do with her, so I kind of just handed her to a friend. At the studio where we do a meet and greet on the Sunday – it's packed, it's really busy and they're pushing each other. I said, 'Are you all right?' and gave her a hug and I was like, 'Oh, oh, lovely, thank you,' and put her back."

All those who had any connection with him were delighted with the association, rushing to congratulate Jaymi and his new friends. Helen Beauchamp, Putteridge High School head teacher, said: "As Jaymi was a former student the whole school is very excited about Union J and we are all keeping our fingers crossed that the town will do the right thing and give them the support they deserve. We all wish them the very best of luck this weekend."

She wasn't alone in wishing them well. Local council leader Hazel Simmons said: "It's fantastic that local lad, Jaymi Hensley, with his band, has got this far in the competition but they now need the town's support so they stand a chance of becoming this year's winners."

They didn't become the winners, but they certainly got the support. Luton was getting thoroughly overexcited about one of its sons doing so well. Many locals knew Jaymi personally and many who didn't had been aware that he'd tried *The X Factor* before and were now thrilled that his career suddenly seemed to be taking off. Another element of a show like *The X Factor* is that it gives many local communities a personal sense of participation. It was as if Jaymi wasn't just competing on his own behalf but for all of Luton, and they were right behind him all the way.

After Union J left *The X Factor*, there was some regret – but as we now know, they didn't actually need to win to benefit from the show. There was still a huge amount of goodwill and great excitement about what was to happen next. It even made the Putteridge High School newsletter, *Headteacher's News*:

It has been an exciting term for successes of past students.
Jaymi Hensley came so close to winning *The X Factor* with

his band Union J and, when the band were voted out, we
missed out on a chance for the band to visit the school
with Louis Walsh, which was disappointing for all – there
is no doubt that Jaymi and the band have a successful
career ahead of them.

Because Jaymi is the second oldest member, with a dominant
personality, he is sometimes taken to be the lead singer, which is
not exactly the case. But it is widely acknowledged that he has a
very good voice, as well as possessing the charisma which is
crucial for any singing star. As time went on though, and the
spotlight shone on him fiercely, Jaymi began to realise it was
inevitable that people would start asking questions about boyfriends and girlfriends. When he had previously been in *The X
Factor*, he hadn't got far enough to excite anyone's curiosity. But
now everything had changed, and it wasn't just a case of a few
people asking questions: there had been the interview in *Bent*,
which made the true state of play pretty obvious, as well as
footage on the internet of Jaymi flanked by two male dancers.
Clearly, something had to be said.

And so Jaymi made the momentous decision which promptly
made life much easier for him. There was no longer the fear that
a story would 'out' him before he was prepared. Living a lie,
whatever the circumstances, is difficult and miserable, and now
that the truth was out in the open Jaymi had nothing to fear. It
hadn't altered his standing one iota – girls were still screaming at
him and he made the Sugarscape Hottest Lads of 2012 list,
coming in at number 41.

In some ways it's fair to say that British audiences have always
warmed to gay entertainers, even if the gayness was not spelled
out as such. Think of old comics like Frankie Howerd and Larry
Grayson whose sexuality could not really have been in doubt to

anyone, even if it wasn't as open as it would be now. But Frankie and Larry had never been in danger of gracing anyone's 'hottest hunks' list, and it was rare that someone gay could be classed as a heart-throb (with possible exceptions like Rupert Everett). Even the flamboyant and very good-looking Rylan Clark was not spoken of in quite the same way – he was more of a gay celebrity as opposed to a celebrity who just happened to be gay. It may have been a fine line, but Jaymi had broken new ground in some ways and was very relieved to have done it.

Some weeks later, Jaymi revealed to sugarscape.com just what an enormous relief it had been:

> I've been getting an absolutely amazing reaction since I came out. From female fans and from young guys struggling with their sexuality. That's the main reason I did it. I was in a stage when I was younger and I didn't have anyone to look up to. I always wished there was someone honest and open about it and I thought, who am I to sit here and not give that to these kids. I've had amazing responses from young guys saying, 'Oh, I've now had the courage to tell my family,' I had one girl tell me her brother was really depressed and in a really bad place before I came out and seeing me do that, he's told his sister and they've bonded over it. It's been an amazing experience and I feel like I've helped people.

It would be easy to dismiss Union J as just another boy band who got lucky, but they were now encouraging a form of social responsibility that influenced their fanbase and actually worked as a force for good. The open acceptance of Jaymi's sexuality, his self-proclaimed happiness and the fact that it was absolutely not an issue for the rest of the band (nor anyone else really) was having an impact on the wider culture.

Union J repeatedly praised Jaymi for his bravery in coming out, told everyone how proud they were of him and, in doing so, pulled a few more barriers down. These boys were having an influence on very young fans and were helping to stamp out whatever prejudice might remain against gay people. As a consequence, young men (and women) in a similar position to Jaymi were finding the courage to come out themselves; the more he spoke about it, the easier it got.

The ramifications didn't end there either. In February 2013, Jaymi featured in a Radio 1Xtra documentary hosted by DJ Adele Roberts, herself gay, about what it was like to come out just as his career was taking off. Other people taking part included Frank Ocean and Stooshe, who were both out and proud. Jaymi gave an honest account of his own life, why he decided to come out when he did and the impact it had on his own and other people's lives. The very fact that the documentary was on the sister channel to the BBC's popular Radio 1 was in itself an indication of how much had changed, given its honest account of what it was like to be gay, strong theme and strong language.

"I've always known, always," Jaymi revealed in his interview, before going on to say that he'd had girlfriends, of sorts, because he enjoyed hanging out with girls. But ultimately, of course, his feelings lay in a different direction, and it was when he was still a young teen that he had a conversation that explained to him what his feelings meant. It was a life-changing moment of self-discovery, setting him on track for the person he was going to become.

"I remember when I was about 14, I was talking to someone who went to Sylvia Young in London and he was talking about someone who was gay, and I thought, 'That's what it is,'" he explained to the interviewer. "Attitudes have changed a lot since I came out, but I've got a very normal, 2.4 children sort of a life, just with a man."

Jaymi credited the fact that he came out when he was very young as helpful for his family, as it might have been a little more difficult to deal with if he'd left it till full adulthood, or even early middle age. Certainly, his family appeared to adopt an exemplary attitude, offering nothing but support and encouragement, and, if truth be told, not feeling too much surprise.

But Jaymi's situation was a little unusual, in that he in effect had to come out twice – once in his teens to his family and friends, and then again to the wider public when he appeared on *The X Factor*. The show played a role in all of this too. To be cynical, no one who had anything to do with the programme was averse to drumming up as much publicity as possible, and Jaymi's self-outing had certainly done that. For a few days afterwards, it was scarcely possible to open a newspaper without reading an account of it.

But there were other factors. After all, Louis Walsh was gay and must have been pleased about the fact that someone could now live their life openly and honestly, without the fear that everything could be destroyed if the truth were to out.

And then there was the role model element. Jaymi spoke about how different it would have been if he himself had a gay role model in a boy band when he was younger, who he might have been able to fancy. While he didn't underestimate the difficulties involved in anyone coming out, he stressed that people would feel stronger and happier if they were able to do so, adding that families would still support their children because family is family – although it must be said that Jaymi had been lucky with his lot, who had been nothing but supportive from the start.

Jaymi followed up with an interview in *Bliss* magazine, in which he announced that he and Olly were engaged. Olly, who had become an enthusiastic tweeter, also had his say: "were [sic] already engaged babe!" he tweeted to one follower. "Jaymi flew me to Rome back in 2010 and proposed to me there! xxx"

The world of boy bands had changed beyond all recognition from several decades previously. Even a few years earlier, this would have been unthinkable. (Jaymi also joked that the outing stuff was all a disguise and that he was actually going out with Ella Henderson. But it's pretty safe to discount that.)

Indeed, Jaymi seemed intent on giving advice to young people. In the early days, when the boys were asked how fans could make an impression on them, Josh recommended a big smile and George went for twinkling eyes, but it was Jaymi who was the most down to earth. "Just be yourself," he said. "Don't worry about being someone you're not. Just come up and be yourself, that's all anyone looks for in a woman." It was sound advice for anyone in every walk of life, something which he'd clearly followed himself.

Some people believe that, in the longer term, Jaymi still harbours ambitions to make it as a solo singer, but the fact is that he fits into Union J very well and as a member of a boy band he has found his niche. His strong personality makes him a dominant factor and his bossiness is a force for good – the boys have a very heavy workload and need someone to ensure the wheels are running smoothly, and that they are all that they want to be.

Jaymi would celebrate Union J's record deal with another large tattoo on his arm. Although the odd ink mark is visible when he's onstage, however, on the whole he stays covered up in front of the fans. His family and his hometown of Luton remain proud of their talented son, and the consensus is that a

141

successful future awaits him. In some ways, Jaymi worked harder than any of the boys to make it through to *The X Factor* and he is now beginning to reap the rewards.

And now for the trivia that emerged as Jaymi came into the spotlight: he likes his Aztec onesie, in which he has been pictured out on the town; he also likes partying, tattoos and the *Twilight* movies; he has a dog, a cat and two goldfish – and a great future ahead.

12

The Funny One

It was July 28, 1992, and the Cuthbert family was delighted. A new arrival had landed in their midst: baby Josh, who was to go on to become 'the funny one' in Union J, or 'Posh Josh'. Josh's parents, Kathryn and Graeme, would go on to have two more children: Callum (seven years younger than Josh) and Victoria, (10 years younger).

Josh's first school – where he was to discover his musical talent – was Cranbourne Primary, motto: "Where learning and friendships grow." Like so much in the area, its roots were deep in the past. There had been a primary school of some form in Cranbourne since 1709, while the current school moved to a red-brick building, now listed, in 1880, next door to the Old Police Station and across the road from the Old Creamery.

★ ★ ★

The small town of Winkfield is a quiet place. With a population of just over 15,000, based near Windsor and Ascot race course in Berkshire, it is a typical English Home Counties location, where the neighbours all know each other and life is lived at a calm pace. It is a place with roots in ancient Britain, its name derived from Wineca's Field (Wineca was a man's name meaning 'little friend'); the village per se was established circa 942AD, when it was founded by a nun named Saethryth.

Although only 30 miles from the centre of London, it retains a country air: local landmarks include Winkfield Manor, built at the end of the 18th century and used as a hunting lodge, and another historically important house called Foliejon – known earlier as Bellestre, it was owned by the 14th-century Bishop of Bath & Wells, John De Drokensford. (Its name was said to have changed when a subsequent owner discovered her footman in compromising circumstances with a local village girl, crying, "This is folly, John!" Rather more prosaically, it might have been so called because the bishop built a folly – i.e. an ornamental building – in the grounds.)

Other noteworthy buildings include Winkfield Place, originally built in the late 17th century and initially the home of the Edwards family, who were closely involved in running nearby Ranelagh School. In 1751, the house was almost entirely rebuilt by its then owner, Richard Buckley, and it now stands as a handsome and imposing residence, used by the Canadian Red Cross during the Second World War and subsequently as a *cordon bleu* cookery school, before being divided into the apartments where some inhabitants of this affluent and salubrious location live.

Elsewhere there are all the normal signs of small-town life. Many of the buildings are listed, including Knights Hall, The Pump Room – which dates from when Winkfield had its own spa – and several local cottages, farm buildings and houses. Various activities are laid on for the town's young, including Karen's Community Café, held once a week for local children to drop in, play sports and buy drinks and snacks at the tuck shop, and a 'teen shelter', which is exactly that – a place for teens to hang out.

The rivals: with District 3.
(COALITION PICTURES LTD/REX FEATURES)

(KP/SPLASH NEWS/CORBIS)

Two into onesie: on *The X Factor* Tour, October 2012.
(MATT KEEBLE/SPLASH NEWS/CORBIS)

(STEVE MEDDLE/REX FEATURES)

Are we related? JJ in Disneyland, Paris.
(REX FEATURES)

Taking the mic: at Comic Relief.
(COMIC RELIEF/SPLASH NEWS/CORBIS)

Yes, it's us! The boys outside the BBC.
(BERETTA/SIMS/REX FEATURES)

Nearby is the Cranbourne Amateur Dramatic Society and Bracknell Forest Countryside Events, which arranges outings in the local green and pleasant rolling hills. In the surrounding area there are leisure and sports centres, numerous golf courses and three churches: St Mary's in Winkfield, St Martin's in Chavey Down and St Peter's in Cranbourne. Opposite St Mary's stands the White Hart Inn, dating from the 17th century, which was once a courthouse – the notorious Judge Jeffreys, known as 'the Hanging Judge', is said to have sat in judgement here. The White Horse pub is now an Italian restaurant, and was once owned by Ray Dorset, the lead singer of Mungo Jerry – because of its proximity to London, towns like Winkfield are very popular with the celebrity crowd.

There is no shortage of local lore. In the 19th century, one lady was reputed to be a witch. When a neighbour borrowed her spectacles and failed to return them, in revenge she apparently turned herself into a squirrel and pelted him with nuts. Her other exploits included turning herself into a hare in order to make trouble with local workmen who were causing too much noise: one of the men set his dog on the hare, who managed to bite it in the leg; the hare only escaped by jumping through a window and the lady herself was later seen nursing a wounded leg.

In short, Winkfield was a pleasant place, resonant with history. It was safe to roam around the nearby parks and outside spaces and there were plenty of facilities for younger people. But not too far away were the bright lights and excitement of London, with its stage schools and musicals all within easy reach. It was the perfect place for an ambitious young performer to grow up.

★ ★ ★

Josh's primary school was host to about 200 children between the ages of four and 11; it also boasts a sports field, playground, swimming pool, conservation area and sports hall, as well as ultra-modern ICT, community room and kitchen facilities. It presents itself as a "traditional semi-rural small school environment".

Inside the building, there are seven classrooms and a hall for assemblies. The school strives (successfully, by all accounts) to create a happy and welcoming atmosphere, and to foster the personal development of its pupils as well as their education. Its uniform is grey and burgundy and, as with all the other children, the young Josh would be expected to look smartly turned out. There were plenty of after-school clubs for the children to join in, as well as extracurricular activities including a choir.

Josh was a popular little boy. Lively and spirited, he made plenty of friends throughout his school days, while life was good all round. His was a privileged upbringing in the Home Counties, quite a different background from the other members of Union J. However, like Jaymi, Josh knew that he wanted to be an entertainer from very early on and he would, in fact, start his show business career much earlier than the rest of them – although it was only when he joined Union J that he really came into his own.

Entertaining was not Josh's only love – he was also a sporty little boy. He was a very talented footballer, joining Ascot United Youth in 1999 and staying with them unto 2010, as he rose through the under-sevens to the under-18s, starting as a goalkeeper and ending up as a young referee in 2011. (His brother still plays for the club.) Pictures exist of the young Josh in training gear and, if his career in entertainment hadn't taken off, there is every chance he would have become a footballer.

Josh realised he was musically talented from early on. When

he was still at Cranbourne, aged just 11, he auditioned for the part of Scrooge in a musical production of Charles Dickens' *A Christmas Carol*, astonishing his parents in the process. It prompted them to take the actions that would launch his career. "I had no idea he had a voice – we were blown away by him singing," Kathryn was later to tell the local paper, the *Bracknell Forest Standard*. "We got him straight into Stagecoach in Bracknell, who told him to audition for *Chitty Chitty Bang Bang*." This he did – and got the part, performing in the role for nine months at the London Palladium. The actor playing the Child Catcher was none other than Stephen Gately, who was later to find fame in Boyzone.

Stagecoach was to prove an invaluable training ground for the young Josh. Part of a chain of 700 theatre schools worldwide, it operated at the weekends and offered drama, dance and singing classes. Today it bills itself as building life skills and confidence, and, while there's no doubt it did that, it also taught Josh the performing arts.

It built his confidence too. Like Cranbourne, Stagecoach had a noticeably cheerful and vibrant atmosphere, the perfect place for a young and ambitious student to thrive. The teachers were all young and enthusiastic, only too happy to encourage the talent they discovered in their midst.

And so the hard work began: Josh began to realise that showbiz was not all glamour but a lot of hard work, with rehearsals, lines to learn and dance routines to memorise. But he was a natural talent who thrived on the challenge and it soon became obvious that he was not just another schoolboy per-former – this one had the potential to become a star.

Josh's secondary school was Charters, in the nearby area of Sunningdale. Billed as a specialist sports and science college, with the motto "Unity, Respect, Excellence", it was a thriving community established in 1958, now a comprehensive of such excellence that, in 2006 and 2009, it was graded as '1 – outstanding' by OFSTED. Nor was Josh its only famous alumnus: other ex-pupils included Chesney Hawkes and Tamsin Green.

Charters catered for children from the ages of 11 to 18, offering a comprehensive academic curriculum as well as numerous extracurricular activities including Ascot Youth Club, the Duke of Edinburgh Awards Scheme, sports, choirs, vocal groups and an orchestra, clubs for specific academic disciplines such as science and geography, debating, gymnastics and chess clubs, creative writing groups, gardening groups and a drama club. Frequently praised by OFSTED for almost all aspects of school life, it strove to teach the children leadership qualities while building up confidence in themselves.

Josh was a cheeky little chap, both lively and a bit naughty, who evokes fond memories today. "Josh is well remembered by staff and some pupils at Charters as a real character, who brought a smile to the face, could be a bit cheeky, but had a sparkle about him," Martyn Parker, co-headteacher of Charters School, told the *Bracknell Forest Standard*.

He was developing a life outside school too. His first job was working in one of the restaurants at Legoland, Windsor, which was nearby, while at the same time his football was coming on apace. Footage still exists on YouTube of Josh playing the beautiful game. Indeed, it was such a passion that he later said he would have been a football player if he hadn't been a singer. But fate intervened.

When he won the role in *Chitty Chitty Bang Bang*, at the age of 14 in 2004, Jason Donovan and Christopher Biggins were also in the cast, alongside Gately. "Seeing Josh onstage was a proud moment for us as a family," Josh's mother, Kathryn, told the *Windsor News*. It was also a moment when they realised, beyond any doubt, that he really did have it in him to go places. Quite how far, of course, they were not yet to know.

No one was more utterly thrilled to see Josh onstage than his grandmother, who went to see him every week. In all she spent about £800 on tickets to see her young grandson – but she felt it was cheap at the price. What with stage school, West End productions and a growing consensus that there was real talent there, it was more than apparent that Josh was cut out for a career in entertainment. The only question was which way he would develop. This was musical theatre, after all, and it was an exceedingly tough profession in which to make any headway.

The future was not assured. Not quite yet.

The next step was to enrol in the famous Sylvia Young Theatre School, where so many famous celebrities in Britain today have learned their trade and which Jaymi was also attending at the time. Josh was there from 2005 to 2007, attending the Saturday school where, alongside 'Singing with Bobby', he took classes in drama and street dance. Acting was still a real possibility at that stage (and may become so again in the future), given that it was amateur dramatics that got him started and a role in a musical required acting ability, as well as being able to sing. At that stage he was keeping his options open, although ultimately music would win out.

Josh himself was becoming pretty sure that he wanted to be a singer and so, aged 15, he auditioned for *The X Factor* for the first time in 2007. Like Jaymi, he'd have some experience of what it was like to go on the show before he joined Triple J. It also meant he knew how difficult it was to get through, and would be well aware of how lucky they all were to have done so.

Kathryn accompanied him that first time around, but it was not a success. "I was his chaperone and it was a very intense experience," she told *Bracknell Forest Standard* when Josh tried again a few years later, at that point with Triple J. "He was probably too young then but he is ready for it now."

He certainly was by then. But *The X Factor* was also where he met Blair Dreelan for the first time and, although they didn't form a close bond, they kept in touch from that point.

Like Jaymi, Josh refused to be disheartened. He began to plan his next career move, at the back of his mind remaining convinced that reality television was the way forward. He also began to contemplate the possibility of working in a boy band. But there was also time for plenty of fun: Josh was a young man out on the town, partying away with the best of them. Sometimes his exploits got a little raucous, as he revealed when appearing in *The X Factor* and when interest in him was beginning to grow. "I've worn a thong before on a night out," he told *We Love Pop*. "Three of my friends did it too, as a dare. But then we did pull our pants down in the middle of a club – I mean our trousers! We pulled our trousers down to show off the thongs. That was the only time I've worn girls' pants. It was extremely uncomfortable."

Josh went on to work in IT sales in order to keep body and soul together, but he knew this was never going to be a full-time career. The performance bug had well and truly bitten by that stage, and by now he was utterly convinced that what he really wanted to do was be in a boy band. He put out feelers to the marketplace – and it worked. His details went onto StarNow, where he announced himself as 5' 11" and 154 lbs, with blue eyes, a 31-inch waist and a shoe size of 9.5. He wanted to join a band, preferably as a lead singer, and had a falsetto vocal range.

His singing style was pop, his favourite genre, and his influences were Michael Bublé, Chris Brown, Blue, Tinie Tempah, Bruno Mars and 'N SYNC.

Josh's first proper outing with a boy band was an outfit called Boulevard, which was formed around the end of 2009 and which he was with for two and a half years, until leaving for Rewind. He had been in a few others, but this was the only one that looked as if it had a serious chance of making it (at least until he met up with the people behind Rewind).

Boulevard was made up of Josh, Andy Rice, Ryan Davis and Alistar Jay, and they had some success to begin with, supporting Boyzone on tour (whose Stephen Gately was known by Josh from the West End production of *Chitty Chitty Bang Bang*). They had come together in the way that so many boy bands do – they had not known each other initially, but when it emerged that they were all after the same thing it made sense to team up. Andy and Ryan were both Irish, as of course were Boyzone, and so although they performed in both the UK and Ireland, they were considered to be more of an Irish band.

"We didn't know each other at first but knew of each other through mutual friends," Andy told the Irish *Independent* in 2011. "We did a sort of audition process and then got together as a band. Between us we like a broad range of music but we sing mostly pop songs and R&B when we're onstage. We've already recorded a few tracks so far and over the next couple of months, we hope to finish it off and then finalise a deal with a label."

Indeed, at that stage it looked as if this was going to be the way in which Josh made it, although it ultimately had the effect of disillusioning him so much that he contemplated leaving the business. By this stage he was practically a veteran of the industry, having been performing professionally since he was 14.

Andy spoke to the *Dundalk Democrat* about the group's intentions and plans for the future. "We knew a while ago that we were going to support [Boyzone] again, but we just had to confirm with them recently that we were still available to do the dates and then they put the word out about it to the various radio stations and people advertising the shows," he said. "We've supported them before in the O2 in London two years ago and all over Ireland and since then we've also done the Childline Concerts with them. They wanted us to go with them on their UK tour as well but we're recording an album at the moment so we could only do a few of the dates, but still it's a great honour."

Indeed, while Union J would garner so many comparisons to One Direction, Boulevard found itself compared to Boyzone for obvious reasons. And, of course, Louis Walsh was Boyzone's manager.

Although Union J seemed totally fresh and newly put together in the summer and autumn of 2012, some of these associations and links were longstanding. Even if Josh and Louis had no direct contact at that point, Josh would certainly have known how important a person in the music industry Louis was.

But at that stage, it really did seem as if Boulevard would make it in their own format – they would hardly have turned down some of the dates supporting Boyzone if it had not been the case. A record deal seemed imminent and for the moment it was all go. "We're doing a lot of writing at the moment for the new album and we've been heading over and back to London to work on a few of the tracks," said Andy. "The tour dates with Boyzone should be really good fun. We're preparing for it at the moment and it's good craic. We know the lads very well and they're all really cool and it's pretty decent of them to have asked us back to support them. It should be really cool."

But although Boulevard was to go through several different line-ups, and indeed still exists as a band, for Josh it was not to be. He'd got a taste of what it was like to be in a band and to go out touring on the road, but various promises had been made and not kept. The exact deal he was expecting didn't materialise. All in all, he was left feeling so disillusioned and disappointed that he thought of quitting the music industry altogether.

He was now with his girlfriend, Chess (short for Francesca) Jones, had a job in IT sales and was beginning to wonder if any of it was worth it. As far as he was concerned, a lot of effort had resulted in precisely nothing and he was feeling extremely fed up.

13

Opportunity Knocks

Even if Josh was still not a major pop star, something had come out of his days with Boulevard – Kasey Monroe had seen him perform. By now acknowledged for spotting new talent in the industry, she and Julian White were working to put a group together.

Despite the fact that Josh's hair was still worn around his face, rather than in its later famous quiff, Kasey could see he was exactly what she was looking for. He was a very good looking boy, on top of which he could sing, was experienced and, most importantly of all, exuded charisma. And so, just as he was about to give up on the business altogether, Josh got an invitation to try out for Rewind.

Once the new band had been put together, Josh and Jaymi were initially rather wary of one another – but, having both been to stage school and sharing some professional performing experience, they settled down in the end. Josh became good friends with JJ and fellow band member Ben, but, possibly as a result of his earlier disillusionment, didn't seem to want to put in too much effort. Sometimes, according to Kasey Monroe, people felt as if he wanted it handed to him on a plate. But underneath it all, though, the hunger was reawakening – he'd been determined enough to put all the effort in throughout his adolescence, and now that opportunities were presenting themselves again he was keen to take them. He began to think he might make it after all.

Kasey believes that Josh didn't really want to leave Rewind, not least because he was now good friends with Ben and didn't want to let him down. But still, the three Js would soon become Triple J – and would be managed by Blair Dreelan.

Josh found himself back on *The X Factor* once more. He knew the drill, having been there before, although he was a little older now and with considerably more experience than he'd had the first time round. He also had a much clearer idea of how competitive the industry could be. But like Jaymi, he was determined to give it another go – and so they were off.

In the background of *The X Factor*, there is a whole army of hairdressers and stylists waiting to weave their magic, and, as first Triple J and then Union J began to progress up the greasy pole, they became a focal point. Josh, in particular, was an extremely good-looking guy, and yet it was felt he wasn't quite making enough of his looks.

As the series progressed, Josh's appearance underwent a transformation. His hair went up into a quiff, revealing striking bone structure and cheekbones to cry for. There was more than a passing resemblance to the young Elvis Presley. From that moment on, Josh's hair became a talking point, with him at one stage threatening to grow an Afro (unlikely, it must be said):

"Okay my hair really needs a cut now its been 6 weeks!!!! Wheres @jamiestevens7 when you need him!!! Josh x" he tweeted.

"I'm starting to grow an afro lol"

But it had the immediate effect of turning him into the most sought-after member of the group: all the boys were popular, but his combination of quiff, cheekbones and pout achieved dramatic results. George asserted that Josh got the most love from the fans. "You can't beat a bit of female attention. It's wicked. It's amazing," Josh himself confirmed to *Reveal*.

In some cases that attention was directed straight back again, for Josh also announced of the backing dancers, "They are stunning! Bring on the dancers, that's what I'm saying. I don't think any of them can speak English though – so it's all about the eyes."

It was actually JJ who was to strike up a relationship with a backing dancer – but Josh clearly didn't mind looking.

As had happened with all the boys, Josh's local community threw itself behind him. His school and old football club called on people to support him and Kathryn put up posters calling on people to vote for him, designed by local Berkshire paper *The News*. The whole family then attended Sunninghill Victorian Fayre to help raise money for good causes – by raffling off signed photos of Josh and his Union J bandmates, as well as the other *X Factor* contestants. Even though these were still early days, their star had risen sufficiently for them to be acknowledged as bona fide celebrities who could profit worthy causes.

"We raffled a signed photo of the boys and raised £120, which was split between the Ascot Day Centre, Sebastian's Action Trust and Martha McCarthy, who suffers from a rare chromosome disorder," Kathryn told the *Windsor Express*. "We are also hoping to raise more money for Martha McCarthy at a live screening of *The X Factor* by FASBAT musical theatre group to its members and families, and there will be various competitions throughout the evening." Not for the last time, Union J were becoming involved in good works.

As the series progressed, Josh's desire to make it in the music business returned with a vengeance. Just under halfway through, the boys had come close to being booted out but fought back strongly, prompting an enthusiastic response from the judges. Having been in the bottom two in week four, they "knocked it out of the park", according to Nicole, in week five with a cover of Taylor Swift's 'Love Story'.

Tulisa got it spot on when she said, "Your fans are loads of young screaming girls across the country and all they want to hear is you sing beautiful songs beautifully to them and you nailed it." It was then that Louis told them they could be the "next big boy band".

"We're chuffed to bits," said Josh, all thoughts of quitting the music business now totally forgotten. "Last week being in the bottom two wasn't nice but we've come back fighting and we've given it our all this week. Fingers crossed that came across."

The boys' star continued to rise; Josh, pouting all over the place, was beginning to attract serious attention. He was spotted kissing a mystery blonde on his hotel balcony and, while all of them were now getting mobbed on a regular basis, Josh seemed to exert a particular fascination. He was not only good looking but he had poise and mystery. Kasey had been spot on when she saw his star quality; now it was coming out in spades. Posh Josh, with his affluent Home Counties background, was turning into a bona fide pop star and loving every minute of it. It was all a long way from am dram and stage school.

Fan sites began to appear, both for Union J as a whole and Josh alone. He was tweeting along with the rest of them, but other snippets began to turn up, such as an interview on Tumblr which included the following gems:

If you had the chance to go to Mars, what ONE thing would you take with you?:
"amazing question! I would probably bring my Xbox lol!"

If you weren't singers, what would you be?:
"I would be working in a bakery lol!"

Would you ever date a fan?:
"you never know !!!!"

What's your most annoying habit?:
"my annoying habit is that I snore haha!"

What colour underwear are you wearing right now?:
"I'm wearing black boxers! Ha . . ."

What's your favourite song at the moment?:
"my favourite song is 'don't judge me' by Chris Brown at the moment!"

Do prefer brunettes or blondes?:
"either I'm not fussed :)"

In case you don't win, are you going to stay together as a band?:
"OF COURSE we will stay together!!! No matter what happens on this show we are going to stay together, we are brothers!"

What food are you craving at the moment?:
"I'm craving a dominos pizza!!!! I'm starving!!!"

It was a great relief for fans to hear that there was no chance of the boys splitting up. Indeed, they would have been mad to do so now!

They were becoming a massive sensation. Josh's resemblance to Elvis just seemed to intensify – as well as the swept-back black hair, there were the cheekbones and the hint of amusement around the mouth. Fans were increasingly beside themselves:

increasing local support, increasing excitement was generated by a viewing of any of them – but especially, it appeared, of Josh.

Josh's relationship status has remained something of a mystery. Some believe that he is actually still with Chess, but that both have decided to play it down – Chess' Twitter account is closed to a wider public, which suggests that, at the very least, she doesn't want to be questioned about any relationship, past or present.

And then Ella Henderson gave a mysterious interview to *Look* magazine, which seemed to imply there might be something going on. She seemed very sure of the status quo and Josh would later dampen speculation as much as he could. "Let me explain it like this," she began. "George is my best friend. Jaymi is like my big brother, JJ is hilarious and, yeah, like . . . At the moment it's hard to say. He's still in the competition. As soon as we're both out of it, it's going to go boom. At the moment [we are just] very close and good friends, but after the competition, I'd love to see him. I do want to spend time with him. Only time will tell."

She really was close to all of them, of course, as became apparent when she spoke about her own departure from the show. "I'm so strongly focused on what I want to come out of the competition, but you can't stop how you feel about someone," she said. "I'm the type of person who would look at boy bands and say, 'I wouldn't be interested in that because they're silly and just bothered about the fans,' but those boys are so amazing. [Leaving] was horrible. They were all bawling their eyes out and so was I. I tried to hold it together but I couldn't! I've never experienced a break-up but feeling how it feels to miss Union J, that very slight lost feeling, I can sense how it would feel to break up [with a guy]. But it's exciting now because I get to watch them and I'm rooting for them."

Josh seemed a little taken by this and said that he mainly thought of Ella as a sister. Whatever the real state of play, it should not be forgotten that there are plenty of people who think that, whatever the reality may be, members of boy bands should not openly admit to having a girlfriend, as it might put off the rest of their female fans.

As it stands, Josh is keeping schtum.

When asked directly, George cried, "We're all single!"

"And ready to mingle," added Josh.

Josh was graciousness itself when leaving the show: "I'm so happy with how well we've done," he told Heatworld. And there were some big consolations. "We spoke to One Direction backstage," he continued. "Liam was saying, 'You guys are going to be so successful' and wished us all the best of luck. They're really nice lads. They're like friends, we're getting to know them. We've seen them a few times now. There's no rivalry there at all – we'd love to be as successful as them."

And with that it was briefly back to the parental home. But life had changed for Josh now. He had regained that lost ambition, bonded firmly with his new bandmate George, with whom he was becoming great friends, and had a bright future ahead of him with the band. The disappointments of yesteryear were forgotten and he was raring to go.

Like all of the band though, Josh found it quite difficult to readapt to real life: "It's been really weird not living with the boys this week," he told Heatworld after they had been voted off and then invited back at the end for the finale of the show, when all the major acts appeared. "When I got home I felt a bit lost. We enjoyed tonight, obviously we were gutted it wasn't us in the final three but it's another chance to perform in front of millions so it was great fun."

The smell of the greasepaint and the roar of the crowd had him in their grasp once more – which was just as well, given the schedule the boys now had to stick to. There was to be no hanging about.

After the boys left *The X Factor*, the usual gossip began to emerge about them being lads about town. The dancer Danielle Peazer (who was going out with One Direction's Liam Payne) and Josh had an intriguing exchange of tweets:

"Hairspray tastes awful!!! Lol josh x"

"I don't think you're meant to eat it . . . p.s. this is a public apology for accidentally tripping u up Josh! X" came Danielle's reply.

(Josh was tweeting quite a bit: "Just got smacked in the bloody head by a pigeon at the station and everyone laughed lol :[josh x," was another gem.)

All the boys brought something unique to the band. In Josh's case, apart from the cheekbones (George's are prominent too), it is his prior industry experience and ready wit. He is known as the entertainer of the group, the joker who helps to lighten the atmosphere. But he is as determined to seize the opportunities now on offer to him as all the others are.

Josh even went one further, telling *Heat* magazine: "I'm not sure it's possible to be any bigger than One Direction, but that would be amazing – that would be the dream."

They were upping the stakes. A few years previously, none of them could have dreamt of getting this far: now that they had done so, they wanted to achieve even more.

And so to the trivia about Josh: he is the loudest member of Union J and he swears a lot; he is the most romantic one and can sing 'Hero' in Spanish; he has a cat called Oreo; he once had food poisoning and had to stay in bed for 36 hours; he fancies Jade Thirlwall from Little Mix.

And, as noted above, he distinctly resembles the young Elvis Presley. If he matches Elvis's success, he will go far indeed!

14

A Deal Is Done

It was the first week of December and the semi-final of *The X Factor*. Now there really was all to play for. Just four acts remained: Christopher Maloney, Jahmene Douglas, James Arthur and, of course, Union J, a band that hadn't even existed until a few weeks previously. This time there was to be no final show-down: the act that left would be the one that garnered the smallest number of public votes. The atmosphere and antici-pation had been building up backstage. This was it.

Union J gave it their all: they sang 'Beneath Your Beautiful' and 'I'm Already There', but to no avail. They picked up the least votes but took it in good spirits, wishing their fellow con-testants well and singing Taylor Swift's 'Love Story' as a finale, as well as being joined by their mentor, Louis Walsh, onstage. "I'm a little disappointed, but we were ready for it," he said. "They're going to be the next big boy band." He was right.

Union J were out of *The X Factor* – although it was later revealed that Chris Maloney only beat them to the final by 0.6 per cent of the public vote. Not that it mattered in the slightest. They clearly had a future ahead of them and the next step was to decide what shape it would take – who to sign with, what the first single release should be and all of the argy-bargy that occurs when major new talents hit the scene. The boys themselves were beyond excitement. Until now, they were only getting a taste of what it was like to be a celebrity. Now it was to be the real thing.

No matter how artless boy bands appear onstage, when they chat to the fans or are caught hanging out in nightclubs, in reality a huge amount of work goes on behind the scenes to present them at their best. This had already started when Union J appeared on *The X Factor*, with stylists advising them on what to wear and transforming Josh's appearance by getting him to change his hairstyle. Now a great deal more was at stake. If the boys were going to capitalise fully on the enormous opportunities now open to them, the best professionals in the business were needed. They all duly came onboard.

Manager Blair Dreelan was to play a crucial role in guiding the boys forward at this early stage. He had already set up @UnionJworld on Twitter, which had promptly attracted almost a million followers, while the boys all tweeted separately as well. Now he had to work out not only the direction the band should take, but also how to differentiate them from the group to whom they were so often compared.

It was both a blessing and a curse. If Union J followed One Direction's career path to date then they had a massive journey ahead of them, yet they were not just clones but a successful group in their own right. Then there was the small matter of District 3, who were also preparing to launch themselves at the public, having built up quite a following when they appeared on *The X Factor* and attracted various record companies – were there similarities there, too?

"I can understand the comparison of One Direction and Union J because of the types of band they are," Blair said in an interview with sugarscape.com, in which he was keen to emphasise that not only was there room for all these different bands, but that their musical output was totally different. "But District 3 are very, very much into their R&B and their R&B harmonies, and I think that as a boy band they're going to go in very, very different directions to where we are. At the end of the day the fans have got to go with where their heart is, and I understand that everybody has a loyalty ethic but this is not a war, this is music. You don't compare One Direction to Jessie J because she's a female solo artist – at the end of the day she's still singing pop records. You know the boys are going to come out and do pop records. You either like them or you don't like them, that's how it works with everything really."

It had already happened many times, as Blair knew from his own experience. The really successful ones were those who ploughed their own furrow. They just had to stand out from the crowd.

"I mean I think that you know if you look at the history of boy bands every boy band is compared to the next," he continued. "You know when there was New Kids On The Block right back in the day, Take That were constantly compared to them, then when Boyzone came out they were constantly compared to Take That and then Westlife to Boyzone, and it's just a chain reaction that seems to constantly reoccur. The fact of it is that they're a collective of good looking boys that sing songs, how could you not compare them? One Direction are amazing so if the boys could have a quarter of their success then we'd be over the moon. If anything it's actually quite an honour to be compared. It's a big glove to fill and the boys probably quite like it. I quite like that they get compared to them because like I said it's an honour."

The fact remained that Union J were a band in their own right.

In the meantime, post-*X Factor* life had begun. There were new disciplines now and a different rhythm. It was imperative that the boys continued to rehearse and perform, but there was no longer a big weekly show to aim towards. Instead, they were getting ready for professional concerts. Although they'd had plenty of experience of performing in front of audiences, they had been within the specific confines of reality TV. Now it was going to be the real thing.

The show had dominated the boys' lives for months now and they had to get used to being on the outside again. It took some doing. For all the pressure they had been under, it had become a way of life and they felt the loss, as became apparent from the odd moment of vulnerability: "I do miss my buddie @jahmenedouglas x" tweeted George.

Josh took to Twitter too: "Xfactor has been amazing . . . had a whale of a time," he tweeted. "Thankyou to every1 and so happy for James and Jahmene. Thanku to everyone who voted. Josh x"

The feeling appeared to be mutual. "@UnionJworld Miss you too! x keeeeep smiling and in other news . . . It's mighty cold outside x" replied Jahmene.

Such other touching exchanges also highlighted how the boys were still very young to cope with such a huge change in their lives. It wasn't that they'd gone straight from the parental home into the limelight, but even for people of mature years, such a huge change in circumstances can be overwhelming.

Fortunately, in each case, the boys had very supportive parents, as well as a management company that didn't want them to go off the rails. But they could be forgiven for feeling bewildered: one moment up-and-coming hopefuls, now major stars; even people who have been famous for decades sometimes find the constant attention difficult to cope with. Union J had only become known within the last couple of months.

It didn't take long for the wheels to begin to turn. The boys signed a record deal with Sony, which they confirmed during a gig at Cardiff club Pulse and then went on ITV's *Daybreak* to discuss.

It was nearing Christmas, so the boys burst out of a snowman, each wearing a brightly patterned Christmas woolly jumper. "It's amazing. It's been a crazy week," said Jaymi. "Obviously when we came out of the show the dream was to get a record deal and we're going to Sony today to sort out all the contracts and stuff. Before Christmas we will have our deal finalised."

In the event it was to take a little bit longer – it was not until the end of January 2013 that the contracts were formally drawn up between the boys and RCA, a division of Sony Music Entertainment. RCA was accustomed to dealing with *X Factor* alumni: their other signings included JLS, Alexandra Burke, Aiden Grimshaw and Jahmene Douglas. Syco, Cowell's record company, was also a subsidiary of Sony, but there was a good reason the boys chose to go elsewhere. Not for the first time it involved You Know Who – who were no longer just something to aspire to, but the competition.

"We were told we could chat to any Sony label but One Direction are signed to Syco, so we thought it would be good to sign to a rival," Josh told the *Daily Star Sunday*. "We thought they would fight for us more and it would be good for everyone to have a healthy rivalry. RCA have seen how successful they and The Wanted have been and want the same for us."

Union J didn't want to risk being overlooked by executives at the label itself. Out of sheer competitive instinct, it was the sensible path to take.

Indeed, the plans for the boys' future were getting more ambitious by the day. One Direction and The Wanted (who had also been pitched as rivals as they sprang onto the scene, with the former seen as the winner) had both managed to do what only a few British boy bands had achieved before them – they had cracked the United States. Many had tried and very few had succeeded, but it really seemed there was a possibility that Union J would manage it.

It was yet another factor that had to be taken into account when planning their future direction – they had to cater to the US market as well as the UK. The two were subtly different, but if Union J cracked the States then the world really was their oyster, as the boys all knew.

"We are recording songs they think will work in America as well as the UK," Josh revealed. "The plan is to go international quite early on."

It was another case of striking while the iron was hot, although in this case the urgency was dictated by the success of two other boy bands. If the United States audience was receptive to British boy bands at that point in time, then the sooner the next one was introduced the better. At the same time, however, it was imperative that they chose the right material – and that was a choice that couldn't be rushed.

But Union J had to be kept in the public eye. Indeed, no time had been lost in getting them onstage and the boys were now performing at gigs up and down the land, initially in slightly smaller venues. No one displayed nerves, each took to the stage as if to the manor born, and they continued to gel perfectly together as a group. Their onstage charisma shone through: they came across partly as polished performers, partly as a group of lads larking around and loving it. Many of the numbers were already familiar to their audience, having been performed on *The X Factor*, but this familiarity provoked an even warmer response. They managed to be spontaneous, while coping with an even more overheated fan reaction than usual. It was as if they had always been in their current line-up and George had been there from the start.

The line-up really did work – each of the boys brought something fresh to the mix. Josh had a smouldering quality, JJ was as laid-back as it was possible to be, Jaymi was lively and George looked like the boy next door crossed with a Hollywood star. It was almost inconceivable that he had ever been the plump boy at the back of the class: his impish charm, combined with innate talent, focused all eyes on him as soon as he walked onstage.

And he was doing a lot of that now. Alongside the concerts were promotional appearances and frequent visits to the television studios. All the elements to prepare them for even greater stardom in the future were moving into place.

The boys were allowed a little time off, however. No one wanted them to burn out before they had even got started, and so they returned to their respective homes to spend Christmas with their families, before what would become one of the most hectic times of their lives.

There was so much to be taken into account: on the one hand, everyone wanted it to be the start of a long-term career, but on the other, public interest in the group was currently at a high. There was a sense that their management should act now, before people started to forget them.

Under normal circumstances, the gigs would have been the

way a band would make its name, building up a fanbase and learning their trade over time – as Josh was prepared to do with his time in Boulevard. But in this case the fanbase already existed and the boys were already household names.

Despite their time on the show, they had not gained a lot of experience of performing together live – indeed, they had only existed in their current form for a few months – and so the gigs were, in their way, a rehearsal both for the larger *X Factor* tour, which would begin later in January 2013, and their own tour, which would happen later in the year. That they were already big enough to headline a tour in their own right was astonishing: it took most bands years to get this far.

The excitement they generated was getting wilder by the day. After an appearance at the Buttermarket nightclub in Shrewsbury, their car was swamped by overexcited fans, so much so that they needed a police escort to get off the premises. While it might have looked exciting, such circumstances could quickly turn dangerous. A couple of years previously, Robert Pattinson had nearly been run down by a taxi in New York when being pursued by over-enthusiastic fans, and One Direction had also been put in danger when they were mobbed. Security was now a real issue, although the boys put a brave face on it all.

Union J also performed at the prestigious G-A-Y venue in London, receiving a rapturous reception from the audience when they performed some of the covers they had sung on the show, before getting showered with confetti. They were becoming known for venturing to the edge of the stage and grasping fans' hands, to the delight of the audience who were just as excited as Union J's young teen fans.

This was the kind of reception that could turn a person's head, even leading to possible self-destruction. It was a big danger for young stars when they got their first break. It could lead to a tendency to forget that, no matter how much talent they may possess, they were also dependent on a great deal of luck. More than one boy band had imploded in the past when they started behaving as if success was their divine right.

It was something to be avoided at all costs. Soon after, in early 2013, the massively popular Canadian singer Justin Bieber came to Britain and provided an object lesson in how not to treat the fans: he turned up hours late onstage, was spotted with mysterious-looking cigarettes and generally gave the impression he thought it was all beneath him. It endeared him to no one.

Union J did not do any of that. Somehow they were managing to keep their feet on the ground. There were no reports of diva-ish behaviour and no ego clashes caused by one thinking he was more talented or popular than the rest. Despite their getting tired of all the One Direction comparisons, the older band at least provided a template for how to behave − if Union J ever needed a role model, Harry Styles and co were leading the way. They clearly understood how lucky they'd been and weren't going to blow it either.

But events were now moving so fast that it was hard for Union J to keep up with what was happening, let alone with anyone else. In January 2013, they tweeted about why they'd had to postpone an Irish gig: "Recording our first single on Monday! So sorry Belfast but we have to change the gig date, things are moving so fast for us! We'll be back! X"

This was one of the most crucial stages of all. It was essential that the first single was a hit and some very big names in the industry were being asked to work on it.

The boys celebrated by indulging in some more tattoos, an apparent new tradition surrounding boy bands when they leap into the limelight (Harry Styles was already covered in ink). They already had a few between them, but matters were facilitated by having Kevin Paul (whose other clients included Harry Styles and Ed Sheeran, who had become something of a name in the tattoo industry) attend to them. "I have seen Jaymi's big piece on his arm," said Kevin of the complex image covering most of his upper right arm, which went on to comprise musical notes, stars, the Union flag and much else. "I don't think it was the highest level of work I've seen, but I think he wants me to carry on his arm and do some more on it. I spoke to JJ, we've done his artwork already. I'm on tour with them from this week, so I'll be with them and try and get their artwork ready and take it up to them and discuss it, so we can get them booked in one by one. A lot of them are quite music-y themed. A lot of people like the traditional look too."

But big business still came first. The next step was to look for further management. Blair Dreelan was fine, but the group was now so big on a global level that further help was needed. There had been some talk about Louis Walsh taking them on, which would have made sense in many ways, as not only was he their mentor on the show, he was also one of the world's experts on managing boy bands. But nothing ever came of it. Nor did rumours that they were going to sign up with Oritsé Williams of JLS. In the event, Union J opted to go with Crown Talent and Media Group, who also represented Jessie J and Sugababes, and were very experienced in dealing with the teen market. The company was headed by chairman Marc Marot, a former executive at Island Music Publishing and Island Records in the UK.

The boys returned to *Daybreak*, which was becoming quite a regular port of call (at one stage in the future, their old friend Rylan went on to be a guest host and welcomed the boys onto the show). "We've met loads of managers since coming off the show," said Josh. "We love Louis; [he] was incredible for us during the show."

"It was great to get feedback from someone who's been in a boy band," said Jaymi. "And I think when we came out of *The X Factor*, and we were looking for new management it was really important we made the right decision so we wanted to see as many people as possible, weigh up all the pros and cons. We have made a decision and we're extremely happy with it. We're now with Crown management."

There was other news too: the boys would be embarking on the *X Factor* tour and were beginning to work on that debut single. "It'll be exciting to see everyone again . . . It will be amazing to do it in a huge arena as well," said JJ of the tour, although things had changed slightly since leaving the show – they were now arguably as big a name as the actual winner, James Arthur. But once again, it would be a good opportunity to hone their performing skills.

Josh added of the single: "It's something we wanted to do for years and years. We're so excited and will hopefully record an amazing song." The boys themselves, of course, had only been together as a band for months, but each had harboured the dream of becoming a pop star for a long time now. The dream was finally going to come true.

The boys' mini-tour of smaller venues continued. Matters did not, however, always go totally smoothly. Some dates had to be cancelled when George had an accident, the nature of which was never fully revealed. He ended up having to go to hospital, although he remained cheery as he did so:

"So sorry to everyone in Ireland," he tweeted. "I have had an accident so we won't be able to perform tomorrow so our gigs have been pulled. Sorry . . . I'm fine [I] just had an accident and won't be able to perform tomorrow, I will be fine in a week or so."

But of course, the fans were greatly disturbed. Rumours began to circulate that George had been seriously injured. The mystery surrounding the exact nature of the accident didn't help; with speculation mounting, the rumour that gained the most credence was that he somehow managed to burn himself. More and more fears were voiced for George, so much so that Blair was forced to take to Twitter himself:

"Won't be performing at the show tmrw, but will be back in a week or so!" he tweeted. "Guys it's not serious, please do not worry, just a small accident! George will be fine and back in action real soon! Shows to be rescheduled."

But it didn't calm the fans, who were beside themselves. Union J had hardly got started. Might it now be possible that their future was in doubt?

More calming down was needed. Mark Sutton from Crown Talent and Media Group decided to have his say:

"OK, let's put this to sleep I can tell you George had to attend hospital after receiving a nasty injury his [sic] not dead or dying as speculated. He's fine," he tweeted. The boys also tweeted their support for their bandmate and reassurances to the fans, although the exact nature of the accident was still not made clear.

George made a speedy recovery and matters returned to normal. But the attention the incident garnered, the concerns expressed and the media coverage served to illustrate just how much the boys' lives had changed.

Only time will tell how long Union J will stay together (though there's a good chance it will be for a long time), but it is experiences like these that either bind a band together or tear them apart. Only JJ, Josh, George and Jaymi know what it's like to be in such a position at this point, and so it has formed a bond that only they could really understand. Close as they may be to family and friends, no one else can really understand quite what it's like to have become the focal point of so much attention.

Whether or not they realised it, the boys needed each other's support – because matters certainly weren't going to calm down anytime soon.

15

JCats

By now rehearsals had started for the forthcoming *X Factor* tour, the second stage of the band's leap to centre stage – their own major tour being the third. There was some amusement when it emerged that one of the backing dancers on the tour was Danielle Peazer, the girlfriend of One Direction's Liam Payne. Amusement turned to bemusement when word went out that Danielle was dispensing some form of relationship advice to the boys – according to her, Josh had a "kind of girlfriend" and JJ "likes someone".

Could his "kind of" girlfriend be Ella Henderson? As we have seen, speculation about the two of them would not entirely go away, whatever they said. Josh had said in the past that he thought of Ella as a sister, but she had been quite open about her admiration for him. Neither had been prepared to say, but the air of mystery didn't hurt them – as long as it kept people interested in their lives.

They had to keep some things private. The attention the boys were receiving by now surpassed anything that had gone before. Girls would do anything to get to their idols, and so *We Love Pop* asked George if he would ever date a fan. His answer surprised many:

"No. Because the fan world is close knit and word spreads

really fast between them. And then they'd hate the band and stuff. So it's just easier not to date a fan."

There was some disappointment about this, but what he said made total sense. For a start, the fans themselves tended to be rather unforgiving when a boy-band member got a new girl-friend. Almost every woman Harry Styles had dated (and there were quite a few of them by now) had been absolutely vilified online, and George was actually saving any putative girlfriends from becoming the object of such hatred too. Secondly, Union J had a clean-living image and there was something unwholesome about band members who preyed on the women who idolised them. Stories were rife in the industry about predatory band members spotting a girl in the audience and sending their minders to invite her backstage. There was no chance of Union J going down that route.

It was much better to keep the two areas of life separate, and anyway, George was young, free, single and enjoying himself. The 'romance' with Ella turned out to have been pure specula-tion – indeed, she revealed that the one she actually fancied was Josh and, after Danielle Peazer's remarks, there had been further speculation about the two of them – Josh was spotted out in the early hours, leaving the nightclub Mahiki and holding hands with a mystery blonde.

Meanwhile, he rather ungallantly told *Now* magazine that a romance with Ella was not on the cards. "That'd be odd," he said. "I'm just like her big brother. I heard a rumour about what she was meant to have said, but I haven't spoken to her about it. I'm being honest. I was dating someone from home but it wasn't serious and it was never really going to work out while I was doing the show. So at the moment I'm unattached and up for anything."

In fact, the only one of the group who was in a long-term relationship was Jaymi, whose bond with Olly was going from strength to strength.

Of course, none of this was going to hurt the boys in the eyes of the fans. In the past, it may have been considered career suicide for members of boy bands to have girlfriends – in the early days of Take That, for example, girlfriends were certainly not part of the scene. The fans liked to think of their idols as available and, if there was a female lurking in the background, then they certainly were not. However, that had begun to change in recent years: Harry Styles never seemed to be without a girlfriend, although in his case the turnover was so fast that One Direction aficionados could always hope they'd be next in the queue. At any rate, it was slightly ironic that the only settled member of Union J was the one who was gay – the admission of which would have been unthinkable just a generation earlier.

Indeed, just how relaxed everyone was about it was illustrated via a photograph that appeared on Twitter. Although Jaymi was the gay one, the picture showed JJ in what appeared to be an embrace with Rylan Clark. Both were shirtless and JJ appeared to be biting Rylan's neck.

"Sorry girls . . . Me and JJ @unionjworld have something to tell you . . . X," Rylan tweeted mischievously, but then added: "For all the girls crying, don't stress . . . Only joking ;-) x."

The fans breathed a collective sigh of relief. Rylan was only maintaining his friendship with the boys. Meanwhile, he was doing pretty well himself, having won *Celebrity Big Brother*.

By this time, the fans had a name for themselves: just as One Direction had Directioners, so Union J now had JCats, with forums and fansites springing up all over the net. One fansite, unionjworldnews, asked the boys what they thought of them.

"I absolutely love our amazing JCats," said Jaymi. "They've completely changed our lives forever and [we] will forever be grateful for everything they've done for us! Love you guys sooo much! xx"

George was equally fulsome. "Not only are our JCats the best and most supportive people in the world, they are part of our extended family!" he said. "I love you all so much!"

As for JJ: "JCats mean everything to us. I always say this but without them we wouldn't be where we are now. They are sooo supportive in every step we take and put a stamp on the word loyal. We love you sooo much. Thanks for making our dreams a reality and supporting us so far. JJx"

And Josh: "JCats mean more to me than my fridge at home," he declared. "(My fridge is important because I love coco pops – you need the cold milk from the fridge!!) They are the best set of fans in the whole universe and we can't thank them enough for everything they have done for us so far."

(Confusingly, the younger and newer fans were not called JKittens, but 'bananas'.)

In the meantime, the big guns of the pop world were being wheeled on to help guide Union J's new single and album. The brains behind One Direction had also got involved with the new boys, as it was absolutely crucial that they got the first single right. Details were gradually being released to help build up the public's expectation, bit by bit – in another teasing interview on Scottish radio, George revealed that the title of the single started with a 'D'.

"I think the plan is to release a couple of singles and then the album will come later," Josh told *We Love Pop*. "We need to find our sound. It's quite hard in *The X Factor* because you need to be quite generic as it's all about song choice."

Indeed. On the plus side, it had given them the chance to try out a wide range of different vocal styles, experience that could only stand them in good stead in the longer term.

But there was no denying that they had to find their style now. "We've been in the studio with Steve Mac and Wayne Heffner," George said. "They've written everything, like JLS's 'Beat Again' and One Direction's 'Gotta Be You'." And, with any luck, something that would turn into a massive hit for Union J.

There were other considerations, as Jaymi noted: "It's massively important to us to get involved with the writing too."

It certainly was, and not just for personal fulfilment or artistic credibility. The person who writes the songs stands to earn massively more from royalties. That had been one of the many factors in the initial break-up of Take That: in the early days, only Gary Barlow had been accredited with songwriting and the fact that he earned considerably more than the rest of them caused resentment in the end. When the band re-formed, one of the conditions was that they were all given songwriting credits and treated more equally, which made everyone a lot happier. The industry had learned from that: if bands were to survive in the longer term, it was best to avoid these fault lines from the start.

★ ★ ★

Finally, the moment that everyone had been waiting for arrived. The boys had played the smaller gigs: now they were ready to take on a bigger challenge and would do it in the company of old friends.

On January 26, 2013, the *X Factor* tour began in Manchester and ran for just over a month, ending in Belfast, Northern

Ireland. It was very good practice for the boys. They were able to perform in front of live audiences and interact with one another onstage – and it was now a considerably bigger stage – but at the same time share the arena with some of their chums from the show, notably James Arthur, Jahmene Douglas, Christopher Maloney, their old friend Rylan Clark, Ella Henderson and District3. Given that everyone involved had already spent months in each other's company, it was an ideal way for them all to make the transition from smaller shows to a bigger tour.

The concerts went on to garner good reviews. Indeed, Union J were not the only stars to emerge from *The X Factor* that year. Ella "stole the show", wrote James Robertson in the *Daily Mirror*. "If there's one thing I learned from spending my evening watching *The X Factor* finalists, it's that they are without a doubt the most talented swines in its history." They were certainly delighting the audience, who were turning out in force.

"It's two months since Simon Cowell's supersized karaoke contest was on our screens and on the evidence of this arena tour, the *X Factor* finalists have been busy," wrote Michael Hogan somewhat waspishly in the *Daily Telegraph*. "Union J have mastered the hysteria-inducing tricks of their template boy band, One Direction. Swindon supermarket worker Jahmene Douglas has cultivated a strange mid-Atlantic accent. Novelty act Rylan Clark has become a bona fide celebrity. And series winner James Arthur seems to have spent the period eating pies." But he, too, conceded that it was good, all-round family entertainment.

Josh Darvill of TellyMix was also in the audience. "Rylan Clark opened the show to possibly the biggest screams of the night with his cover of 'Gangnam Style', and it proved a hit with the crowd," he wrote. "Union J were also loved by the 12,000 strong audience of the MEN Arena, with Josh and Jaymi shining ahead of their bandmates as they sung a cover of Kelly Rowland hit 'When Love Takes Over'." It all boded very well for the future.

Of course, a good deal of larking around also went on. The boys needed it to combat the growing pressure on them as their star rose higher and the music industry predicted bigger things still. George complained (very lightheartedly) to *Top Of The Pops* magazine that Jaymi tended to borrow his clothes, including his boxer shorts, and forgot to give them back. George revealed that he also made a habit of invading Ella's dressing room: "It's funny actually, because I sneak into Ella's dressing room when she's not in there and nick all of her food," he told sugarscape.com. "We have massive platters of fruit and all these snacks, but because all the boys are sharing one room ours goes in like a second. So I just sneak into Ella's room and nick all of her crisps and stuff. Nobody knows."

But the boys were enjoying their time on the road, which was fortunate as this lifestyle would be theirs now for some time to come. "Yes, it's been amazing – it's just like a dream come true," George continued. "We started in Manchester, and obviously it's massive there so it was incredible, and we thought that would be the highlight of the whole thing. Then we started going to some of the smaller venues, like Brighton, that are more intimate. You get to see the fans really close up, and witness their reactions – that was awesome too."

There were no apparent tensions at all between the boys, which was also crucial if they wanted to savour long-term success. "No not at all," George confirmed. "Do you know what – everyone has completely grouped together actually. The dancers are on the bus with us too, and we all mingle and chat to everyone – it's a completely different atmosphere to the show."

To mark Valentine's Day, all four boys gave teasing interviews with *Bliss*. Asked who they had snogged most recently, George bashfully admitted it was his ex-girlfriend – apart from all the people he couldn't talk about. JJ wouldn't tell, but said it was recent. Everyone was a little coy – after all, the entire world seemed to want to know about their love lives now.

They found themselves moving increasingly in show business circles, for the simple reason that only people in similar circumstances could understand the kinds of pressures they had to live with now. George had become great friends with Sonny Muharrem of Loveable Rogues, so much so that the pair decided to move in together.

"George and I have become good mates and we were both looking to share a flat with someone, so we thought, why not?" Sonny told the *Daily Mirror*. "We're doing a lot of the same gigs with our bands, so we can give each other a lift home as well."

They could also give each other a great deal of moral support, given that neither was willing to talk publicly about their private lives. It was a traditional way for two teenage boys to live when they were first starting out – it's just that these two had a rather more unusual life than most boys of their own age.

At heart, Union J were still like most young men of their age – they enjoyed larking about and sometimes behaving outrageously. There was Josh's thong revelation and spotting of band members with unnamed women, although they were careful not to let any details slip out. They had learned to be extremely discreet – in these days of social media, when every phone was also a camera, it didn't do to reveal anything in public.

Alongside *The X Factor* and their own tour, a further series of performance dates began to stack up. Union J were booked to perform at the Sundown Festival in Norfolk, at London's One In The Park gay festival, along with Rylan Clark, at Chester Rocks, at Sound Island Festival in Quex Park, Birchington-on-Sea, at North East Live, alongside JLS at the Stadium of Light.

★ ★ ★

So what does the future hold? Lizzie Catt, editor of the *Daily Express*' 'Night & Day' diary column, thinks they will go on to great things. "It's important that Union J take the time to find their own sound and shake off the label '2012's One Direction'. They may have already been in the studio for new label RCA, part of Sony, but with the single under wraps 'til June, it will be interesting to see what they come up with," she says.

"The boys are keen to point out that they were different to One Direction and more grown up – although the addition of winsome, smiley Harry Styles lookalike George to their carefully coiffed trio at boot camp did mean that, visually at least, they started to resemble the show's 2010 runners up. And with the band targeting a similar fanbase, they'll need to make their mark. They've got bags of personality and they've proved they have fantastic voices that mix well together – with the right songs and strong guidance from Jessie J and the Sugababes management company Crown, they have all the ingredients to come up with something unique.

"Yet while they'll be wanting to stand out from One Direction, they could do well to follow their predecessor's example and bide their time. 1D's number one smash hit 'What Makes You Beautiful' wasn't released until September 2011, when the next series of *The X Factor* was already underway. When I attended the Brit Awards the following February, there were whispers at the swanky Sony afterparty that 1D were on the brink of becoming huge in the States. It seemed impossible but sure enough, they did.

"This slow burn seemed to work terrifically well for 1D, and if Union J can find their niche and take it slowly, there's no reason that they shouldn't replicate that success – especially as Harry Styles and co have helped shift the spotlight onto UK pop, with potential fans all around the world."

Four young men, all with their own hopes and aspirations, and in many cases past disappointments, have all now succeeded beyond their wildest dreams. None could have anticipated how it was going to turn out when they first came on *The X Factor*, and all are still struggling to comprehend the full extent of what has happened to them. A great future awaits them – one which all four are seizing with both hands.

Acknowledgements

Many thanks to:

> Julian White;
> Kasey Monroe;
> Sylvia Young;
> Simon Aylward;
> several people who would speak to me only on condition of
> confidentiality;
> and everyone at Omnibus Press – especially my editor,
> David Barraclough.